IMAGES
of America

WEST POINT
FOUNDRY

The West Point Foundry was located on the east bank (right) of the Hudson River on the sharply pointed cove just below Cold Spring in the Hudson Highlands, about 40 miles from the most northern part of New York City. This detail is from *Map of Putnam County New-York, Surveyed and Published by R.F. O'Connor* (1854). (Putnam History Museum.)

ON THE COVER: On May 1, 1864, a West Point Foundry crew is preparing to prove a 300-pounder Parrott rifled cannon aimed at a Crow's Nest Mountain target on the western side of the Hudson River. Due to their size, few 300-pounders were made, and their use was limited. Parrott cannons of other sizes, both in field and in siege classes, saw widespread use during the American Civil War. (Putnam History Museum.)

IMAGES
of America

WEST POINT
FOUNDRY

Trudie A. Grace and Mark Forlow

ARCADIA
PUBLISHING

Copyright © 2014 by Trudie A. Grace and Mark Forlow
ISBN 978-1-4671-2064-7

Published by Arcadia Publishing
Charleston, South Carolina

Printed in the United States of America

Library of Congress Control Number: 2013939423

For all general information, please contact Arcadia Publishing:
Telephone 843-853-2070
Fax 843-853-0044
E-mail sales@arcadiapublishing.com
For customer service and orders:
Toll-Free 1-888-313-2665

Visit us on the Internet at www.arcadiapublishing.com

In memory of those who lost their lives on both sides
of combat during the American Civil War.

CONTENTS

ACKNOWLEDGMENTS

We are grateful to the many people who, as individuals or as staff members of organizations and institutions, provided information and visual material to us for this study of the West Point Foundry. Of special note is the Putnam History Museum (PHM), formerly the Putnam Historical Society and Foundry School Museum. The museum contributed more than half the images from its extensive West Point Foundry collection.

We appreciate the special insight and photographs that we received from the following people with direct involvement with the foundry's history: Jan Thacher has extensively photographed the foundry's site and worked for years with the PHM's photography collection; Eric Lind, director of the Constitution Marsh Audubon Center and Sanctuary, helped to clarify the US Environmental Protection Agency's cleanup of Foundry Cove and adjacent areas; Stephen Tilly and staff, who directed the stabilization of the 1865 office building on the foundry site, were also graciously helpful; as was Andrew H. Cornell, a descendent of Cornell family members who once owned the foundry.

Staff members at the United States Military Academy at West Point facilitated our research, including David Reel, director of the West Point Museum. Les Jensen, curator of arms and armor, spent hours showing us ordnance. Suzanne Christoff and Susan Lindelmann of the USMA Library Special Collections and Archives provided access to an extensive photography collection from the Civil War era.

For helping us with research and facilitating the use of images, we thank Lisa Nolan, board president of the Society of the Block Island Light; David S. Krop and Claudia Jew, the Mariners' Museum, The Monitor Center; Peter Harrington, curator Anne S.K. Brown Military Collection, Brown University Library; Judy Bolton, Louisiana State University Libraries; Scott Price, the US Coast Guard History Program; Katalina Puig, Para la Naturaleza, a unit of the Conservation Trust of Puerto Rico; and staff of Columbia University's Rare Books & Manuscript Library and Ambrose Monell Library for engineering. We also greatly appreciate images and information about Civil War artillery given by Bernie Paulson from Paulson Brothers Ordnance Corp. and Jack Melton of www.civilwarartillery.com.

The PHM's librarians, Lillian McGinnis and Corinne Giunta, were their usual helpful selves as was Josephine Doherty, a longtime local historian. Mindy Krazmien, director of the PHM, supported and facilitated our work. Linda Faulhaber, our editor, was our mainstay in final editing before manuscript submission.

The images in this volume from the Putnam History Museum are credited, after page 10, as follows: (PHM.).

An asterisk in a credit line indicates a lengthy credit, given here: *Thomas Kelah Wharton diaries and sketchbook, Manuscripts and Archives Division, The New York Public Library, Astor, Lenox and Tilden Foundations (page 17); or *G.H. Suydam Collection, Mss. 1394, Louisiana and Lower Mississippi Valley Collections, LSU Libraries, Baton Rouge, Louisiana (page 23).

INTRODUCTION

The West Point Foundry (WPF) in Cold Spring, New York, in the Hudson Highlands, was established in 1817 as a cannon foundry and was one of the first major industrial sites in the United States. It played a central role in the nation's industrial development, most significantly in the manufacture of artillery and other ordnance but also in the production of many other iron products.

During the War of 1812, several foundries manufactured ordnance for the US government. Efforts were not well organized, nor was production regulated. A British raid on the Principio Iron Works near Havre de Grace, Maryland, in May 1813, underscored the need for coordinated manufacturing of cannons for national defense. In the aftermath of the war, Pres. James Madison called for increased production of ordnance to ensure the nation's security. Three established foundries became new producers of ordnance for the government under military oversight: the Fort Pitt Foundry (1804) in Pittsburgh; the Columbia Foundry, a reworking of Henry Foxall's foundry (1800) in Georgetown; and the Bellona Foundry (1810) near Richmond, Virginia. A fourth cannon-making foundry, the only such private enterprise established after the war, was the WPF, located diagonally across the Hudson River from the United States Military Academy at West Point (USMA, 1802). The site for the new foundry, near what became the village of Cold Spring, was selected for several reasons. Not only was its location a secure one with access to a major waterway, but the area was also rich in the natural resources needed for the successful operation of a foundry—iron ore, wood for fuel and charcoal production, and flowing water for powering machinery.

The foundry was established by members of the West Point Foundry Association, incorporated in 1818, a group of socially and professionally accomplished entrepreneurs led by Gouverneur Kemble (page 14); his brother, William (page 15); munitions expert Brig. Gen. Joseph G. Swift (page 15); and James Renwick Sr., an engineer and professor at Columbia University. Gouverneur Kemble, the major organizational figure, directed operations for many years and was the primary owner. He guided the development of the foundry with great success. His rich social life among major literary, artistic, and military figures of his era (page 80) gives a sense of an extraordinary individual. In 1836, he hired Robert Parker Parrott (page 16), then West Point's inspector of ordnance, and appointed him the foundry's superintendent.

Early on, the WPF primarily turned out ordnance for the military, including various types of cannons, howitzers, mortars, and projectiles. Initial foundry contracts for smoothbore cannons came from the Navy for arming warships and for seacoast cannons, the latter for Army shore batteries. Production soon expanded to other important iron products, including the first American locomotives; marine engines and boilers, both for passenger steamers and for some of the first steam frigates; the first American iron-hulled ship; aqueduct pipes; and the engine and pumps for the US Naval Dry Dock at the New York Navy Yard (later named the Brooklyn Navy Yard). The largest Cornish steam engine in the United States was built by the foundry and delivered to the Jersey City Water Works in Bellville, New Jersey, in 1853. The foundry's market was also international. Beam engines and cane mills were ordered for Caribbean sugarcane plantations. An order came from the Egyptian government for a machine to separate hulls from cottonseed; it was shipped from New York City in 1838.

The foundry's marine engines powered notable ships (pages 22, 23), including the USS *Missouri* (1841), a steam frigate that made the first powered crossing of the Atlantic by a US warships, and the steam frigate USS *Mississippi* (1841), which served as Commodore Matthew C. Perry's flagship in the West Indian squadron on his expedition to Japan in 1854. The USS *Merrimac*, also a steam frigate (later rebuilt as the Confederate ram CSS *Virginia*), was also powered by an engine manufactured at the foundry.

The foundry helped to develop the Cold Spring community; it established a school (page 78) and a church (page 77) and funded six other village churches. Gouverneur Kemble and Parrott each served as local superintendent of the school system and as warden of St. Mary-in-the-Highlands (page 79). During the 1840s, Parrott was a local judge. Under his paternalistic superintendence, the lives of the foundry workers, many of them young immigrants, were heavily regulated. For example, contracts for the apprentices forbade drinking and sex. Parrott owned many houses, some of which he rented to workers, and the foundry paid benefits of a sort to widows and severely injured workers.

Ordnance production expanded at the foundry by 1860 with the manufacture of smoothbore cannons designed by Thomas J. Rodman and John A. Dahlgren. Parrott developed his own rifled cannon design and turned out his first rifle,* a 10-pounder, in 1860. He received its patent the following year. He immediately designed and produced a 30-pounder rifle, which was followed closely by a 20-pounder. These artillery pieces were available shortly after the outbreak of the Civil War in April 1861. In the autumn of that year, the Parrott 100-pounder was produced; the 200-pounder and 300-pounder followed in 1862. In 1864, Parrott's 60-pounder was made for the Navy.

The foundry's output became of critical national importance during the Civil War, with the Parrott rifle, its most important product, in heavy demand. By September 1861, the foundry was manufacturing up to 25 Parrott rifled cannons and 7,000 projectiles per week. When Abraham Lincoln visited the foundry in June 1862, Parrott arranged for him to see the 100-pounder and 200-pounder fired. Parrott had developed a weapon with superior range and accuracy, which could be produced more quickly and more cheaply than any other manufacturer could make it; he had solved the challenges of production engineering and was able to meet the urgent need for rifled cannons in wartime. The sole producer of this weapon and its corresponding projectiles, the WPF received huge commissions from the US government during the war. By the war's end, it had produced more than 2,700 Parrott rifles and more than 1.3 million projectiles of various types and calibers. After the war, the foundry made about 200 additional Parrott rifles.

Parrott's rifled cannons have been the subject of controversy since they were first produced. Claims were made that their design was not his own. Parrott employed the latest cannon-making innovations of the day—namely reinforcing breech bands and rifling—used by other manufacturers, but his patents made no claim to these innovations. He bettered the competition: he developed a simpler gun design with a reinforced breech and, more importantly, a manufacturing process that enabled him to mass produce the weapon. His rifling arrangement of alternating lands and grooves in the bore provided for great accuracy and is also said to have minimized the stresses to the cast-iron tube caused by the spinning of the projectile as it accelerated through the bore. Parrott also made improvements to projectile design and to the methods of applying fuses to projectiles. His developments in ordnance design and manufacture were indeed his own and, with the exception of his rifling configuration, he received patents for his work. The results speak for themselves; no other manufacturer of artillery matched his improvements and production levels during the Civil War.

Controversy arose during the Civil War over the bursting of Parrott rifles in the field. One campaign in particular, the Siege of Charleston Harbor (1863), had a notable share of burst siege rifles, 30-pounder to 300-pounder types. Sand in the beach areas of most batteries sometimes caused obstructions in the bore which then made projectiles explode prematurely, damaging or destroying the gun. Inadequate lubrication to the projectile was also cited as a cause. Friction generated within some shells during firing likewise led to rounds exploding while in the bore; the problem of internal friction was later addressed by coating the shell interior with lacquer or asphaltum. Parrott explains the efficiency and practicality of his artillery pieces in the January 1865 *Report of Committees of the U.S. Senate Second Session 38th Congress, Heavy Ordnance*. His testimony reads in part: "As a new gun, they were considered very successful indeed. At all events, they were looked upon as very much in advance of anything they then had. I do not profess to think they are the best gun in the world, but I think they were the best practical thing that could be got at the time, and I suppose that was the great reason for getting them."

The foundry's fortunes fluctuated during the 45 years following the Civil War, in part because of reduced demand for ordnance and the new competition from steel, which could be produced more cheaply and faster than cast iron. Nonetheless, under the ownerships of Paulding, Kemble & Co. and J.B. and J.M. Cornell Company, a well-established New York City firm, the foundry continued to make many iron products, including heavy machinery, structural columns, metal furniture, and some ordnance. The Cornell output, from 1898 to 1909, involved a step up in that company's production.

When the foundry finally closed in 1911, the buildings were dismantled or deteriorated, although some were used by a succession of other types of companies. Pollution that began with the establishment of a battery plant in 1952 near the foundry site contaminated part of it and Foundry Cove. A US Environmental Protection Agency Superfund cleanup from 1986 to 1996 was preceded by a site study by Edward S. Rutsch and associates completed in 1979. This work was followed by an archaeological study by Joel W. Grossman and associates between 1989 and 1993. After Scenic Hudson Land Trust, Inc., purchased the site in 1996, more extensive archaeological work was done from 2001 until 2006 by a team of industrial archaeologists from Michigan Technological University.

Many WPF artifacts, admired for both their role in the industrial history of America and their designs, are preserved or replicated in museums and at historic sites, primarily in the eastern United States. Replicas of some of the famous WPF locomotives are part of full-scale presentations of the entire trains (pages 19, 20). Lighthouses with WPF iron components at Cape Canaveral (1866; page 86) and Block Island (1875; page 87) are open to the public and partly supported by nonprofit groups. A beam engine and sugar mill (1861; page 122), displayed in motion in Manati, Puerto Rico, is a popular attraction.

Parrott rifles and smoothbore cannons made at the foundry can be found at many historic sites, including National Park Service sites such as Gettysburg, Antietam, Fort Sumter, Fort Moultrie, and Fort Pulaski. An installation of ordnance on the grounds of the USMA includes WPF cannons of several sizes and types. Four WPF-made 10-inch seacoast mortars are set at the corners of the Broome County Soldiers and Sailors Monument in Binghamton, New York. The Watervliet Arsenal, in Watervliet, New York, the site where many wooden field and siege carriages for Parrott rifles were manufactured, has WPF-made objects on view in the arsenal museum. The arsenal is also home to one of eight surviving 200-pounder Parrott rifles. Some WPF guns are famous, including the ironclad *Monitor*'s Dahlgren cannons (page 121) and the Swamp Angel (pages 57, 64), preserved at Cadwalader Park in Trenton, New Jersey.

The site of the foundry is now called the West Point Foundry Preserve and is maintained and made available to the public by Scenic Hudson. The foundry's school (1830), initially for young apprentices, is now enlarged and home to the Putnam History Museum. The museum owns a major collection of photographs, artwork, artifacts, and archival material related to the foundry and is visited by many researchers, including archaeologists and ordnance specialists. The Chapel of Our Lady Restoration (page 126) closely resembles the chapel built by the foundry for its Catholic workers.

Among the relatively rare artistic representations of early American industrialization are two well-known examples that depict the WPF: *The Gun Foundry* (1864–66; page 33) and *Forging the*

Shaft (1874–77; page 88). These large works are in the collections of the Putnam History Museum and the Metropolitan Museum of Art in New York City, respectively. They were painted by John Ferguson Weir, who grew up at West Point, came from an artistic family, and knew the foundry owners. *The Gun Foundry* traveled to Paris for the Exposition Universelle in 1867 and brought Weir admission in 1866 to the membership of the prestigious National Academy of Design in New York City. The work is often reproduced in American history textbooks. In 2007, the painting toured in an exhibition of American art on 300 years of innovation that traveled to China and was organized by the Solomon R. Guggenheim Museum.

Because of popular and scholarly interest in the military history, battlefield sites, and artillery of the Civil War, WPF ordnance continues to receive much attention. It is featured on websites and blogs about the Civil War and is used by reenactors (pages 121, 122). Collectors and institutions avidly acquire Civil War materials, including ordnance and depictions of it. Books and articles on Civil War ordnance continue to be published and can now also be found on the Internet or in digitalized form at museums and libraries. *Harper's Weekly's* Civil War–era issues have been fully scanned and are available for viewing online. Their wood engravings often feature pieces of artillery in action, including many WPF cannon types, at sieges, on battlefields, and on board ships.

The WPF holds an important place in American industrial history, especially in relation to its innovations in ordnance and production methods during the Civil War. Benson J. Lossing, in his book *The Hudson River, from the Wilderness to the Sea* (1866), a best seller of the day and still a popular reference work, conveys the dynamic industrial activity and significance of the foundry at its peak. A walk near the foundry inspired him to write: "Below us we could hear the deep breathing of furnaces, and the sullen monotonous pulsations of trip-hammers, busily at work at the West Point Foundry, the most extensive and complete of the iron-works of the United States."

*The term *rifle* refers not only to the handheld guns used by the infantry but also to the field and siege artillery pieces employed in the Civil War. Helical grooves in the bore of a rifle spun the projectile, giving the weapon increased accuracy and range. Parrott rifles were produced in various calibers (2.9-inch to 10-inch), and these rifles, or rifled cannons, were referred to by the corresponding projectile's diameter (i.e., 10-inch rifle) or its approximate weight (i.e., 300-pounder rifle). The Civil War was the first conflict that saw the widespread employment of rifled artillery.

One

FOUNDING, LOCATION, AND EARLY PRODUCTS OF THE WEST POINT FOUNDRY
1817 TO EARLY 1860S

This is the central section of a painting (1857) by the German-born artist Johann H. Carmiencke (1810–1867), which is one of few works that demonstrates the relationship of the West Point Foundry, Foundry Cove, and the west bank of the Hudson Highlands. The original foundry site consisted of 178 acres of land and 27 acres of marsh. Carmiencke lived in America for the last 16 years of his life. (PHM.)

The foundry's proximity to the United States Military Academy at West Point (USMA) can be seen in a detail from a January 9, 1869, *Harper's Weekly* engraving. From Fort Putnam above the academy, the viewer looks across the Hudson River to Foundry Cove, Cold Spring, and the foundry. Associations between prominent individuals at West Point and the foundry were close for many years. (Mark Forlow collection.)

Cold Spring's business district, Main Street, stands out in this view from about 1900. The road was part of the Philipstown Turnpike, built between 1812 and 1815 and extending to Connecticut, the region's major route east. Raw materials, including wood and iron ore, were transported to the foundry along it. The foundry's dock, the railway causeway, and the foundry are visible at right. (PHM.)

In this view of Foundry Cove and the Hudson, the foundry's 600-foot dock, completed in 1848 and visible in the preceding photograph, can be glimpsed above the right end of the railroad causeway. The causeway blocked boat access to Foundry Cove in 1849, necessitating a new dock. Its length allowed ships with significant draft to moor. Rail tracks ran onto it to facilitate the loading of products. (PHM.)

Sloops are anchored close to Foundry Cove. At various times, the foundry owned sloops and hired others to transport goods by river north to Albany and south to New York City. The New York City journey took about three hours and 40 minutes for the fastest boats. The wide beam of a sloop enabled it to carry large loads. (PHM.)

After a narrow victory in the War of 1812, Pres. James Madison advised that cannons be manufactured for the government at four locations (page 7); prior to the war, cannon production was scattered among several sites without regulation. The site for the WPF, across from West Point, was selected for ease of river transport and natural resources—forests for charcoal production, a stream for waterpower, and iron ore. (PHM.)

Gouverneur Kemble (1786–1875), a well-connected entrepreneur with brief experience as a diplomat, headed the 11-member West Point Foundry Association, incorporated in April 1818. He remained its president until 1836. The next year, he was elected to the US House of Representatives for the first of two terms under Pres. Martin Van Buren. At his death, Kemble was the foundry's principal owner. (PHM.)

William Kemble (1790–1881) was a brother of Gouverneur and one of the association members. He supervised the foundry's New York City Beach Street plant (page 18), where many products were finished, until its operations were moved to Cold Spring in the late 1830s, when he withdrew from involvement in foundry business. His New York City home was on Beach Street. (PHM.)

Joseph Gardner Swift (1783–1865), another founder, was West Point's first graduate and in 1812 became its superintendent and chief engineer of the US Army. He was briefly engaged with the foundry before resigning his commission in 1818 with the rank of brevet brigadier general. This portrait is by John Wesley Jarvis (1781–1839), considered one of the finest portrait painters of his day. (West Point Museum Collection, USMA.)

Robert Parker Parrott (1804–1877), best known as the inventor of the Parrott rifled cannon, which he patented in 1861, was superintendent of the foundry from 1836 until his retirement in 1867. He graduated from West Point third in his class in 1824, became an ordnance officer, and was later responsible for inspecting WPF ordnance production. He resigned his commission in 1836 when Gouverneur Kemble hired him. (PHM.)

This engraving was published in 1821 at the top of a broadside advertising and listing foundry products. (On the broadside, the words "and Boring Mill" were added.) Engraved by P. Maverick, Durand & Co., the scene includes the two-storied boring mill with its flume, the L-shaped molding shop for casting, and a machine for boring cannons (foreground). Without decorative flora, the image was also used on WPF checks. (PHM.)

Thomas Kelah Wharton (1814–1862), an architectural apprentice who emigrated from England in 1830, sketched the foundry and nearby scenes in 1832. This work captures the cove marsh, the gorge in which the foundry was set, and early buildings, including the tall blast furnace (rear) with a waterfall behind it. Wharton (page 77) later practiced in New Orleans. (The New York Public Library.*)

This painting (1865) by John Gadsby Chapman (1808–1889) shows the foundry's 1827 blast furnace, where iron ore was smelted until 1844 when the furnace was shut down. A casting shed is next to it. The furnace may not have been standing when the painting was done. Kemble gave it locally as a wedding present. Chapman was famous for *Baptism of Pocahontas* (1840) in the Capitol rotunda. (PHM.)

An engraving by John Barber (1798–1885), later hand colored, shows the WPF's expansion. At left are the boiler house, its doors open, the molding shop complex (with the tallest smokestack), and a stepped gable building. Another stepped gable structure (right) was the machine shop. Cannons and shot are in the foreground. The work appears in the *Historical Collection of New York State* (1842) by Barber and Henry Howe. (PHM.)

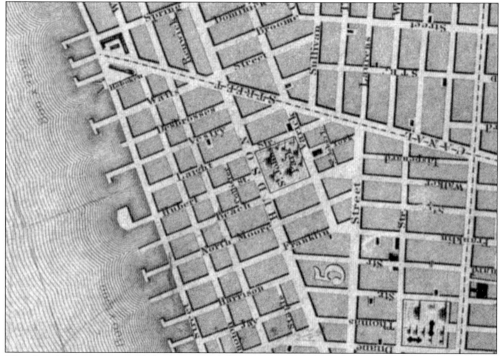

This detail from a map published in 1836 by J.H. Colton shows Beach Street (seven streets below Canal Street between Hubert and North Moore Streets), the location of the foundry's Manhattan finishing plant until the late 1830s. Before landfill was added, Beach Street ended at the Hudson River and had a pier. William Kemble oversaw the Beach Street operations (page 15). (David Rumsey Map Collection.)

In 1830, the WPF produced the first locomotive in the United States, the *Best Friend of Charleston*, for the South Carolina Canal & Rail Road Company. After difficulties with the wooden spoke wheels and a boiler explosion, the engine was rebuilt and renamed the *Phoenix*. Several replicas of the original have been built. One is shown here; another is on display at the South Carolina State Museum in Columbia. (PHM.)

The foundry also manufactured the second American-made locomotive, the *West Point*. Built in 1831, it too was destined for the South Carolina Canal & Railroad Company. This detail of a print, published in the March 5, 1831, *Charleston Courier*, includes a depiction of an eight-piece band of black musicians playing drums, trumpets, and flutes. (PHM.)

The first US locomotive with all-iron driving wheels, the *DeWitt Clinton* was produced for New York State's Mohawk & Hudson Railroad in 1831 from components cast by the foundry. The operational replicas of the locomotive and passenger carriages shown here were created for the 1893 World's Columbian Exposition in Chicago. They are on display in the Henry Ford Museum in Dearborn, Michigan. (PHM.)

The *South Carolina* was the first double-ended locomotive in the world. Designed by Horatio Allen (1802–1889) and built by the foundry in 1831, it had two boilers joined at a central firebox with smokestacks on each end. This design proved impractical—the engine was in continual need of repair—and was abandoned after a short service life. (PHM.)

Designed by John B. Jervis (1795–1885), chief engineer for the Mohawk & Hudson Railroad, and manufactured by the WPF, the *Experiment* (1832) could not generate steam from her undersized coal-burning firebox. Rebuilt the following year with a large wood-burning firebox, the engine was renamed *Brother Jonathan*. More advanced than previous locomotives, the *Brother Jonathan* reached speeds of 60 miles per hour, then a world record. (PHM.)

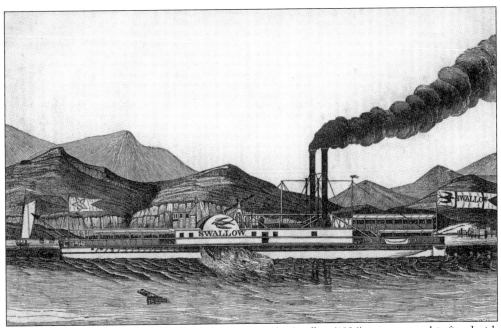

This engraving shows the early Hudson River steamer the *Swallow* (1836), a passenger ship fitted with marine engines and boilers manufactured at the foundry. The *Swallow* operated between Albany and New York City, making the trip in under 10 hours. On the evening of April 7, 1845, she struck a rock near Athens, New York. Of the 350 passengers on board, some 40 lost their lives. (PHM.)

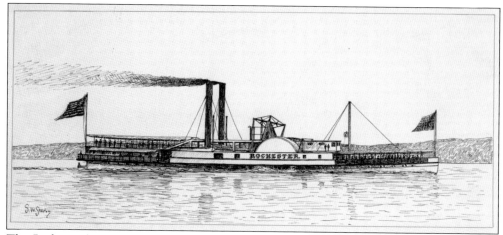

The *Rochester* (1836), a Hudson River steamer that rivaled the *Swallow* for speed, also had a WPF marine engine and boiler. She ran between New York City and Albany until 1852 when she was scrapped. The foundry made engines for other steamers, including the *Erie* (1832) and the *Champlain* (1832). The drawing is by Samuel Ward Stanton (1870–1912), who was lost with the *Titanic*. (Collection of the New-York Historical Society.)

Fitted with WPF marine engines and boilers, the USS *Missouri* (1841), a steam frigate, was the first American steam warship to cross the Atlantic and one of the first built in the United States. While she was moored at Gibraltar on August 26, 1843, an onboard accident set the ship ablaze; her powder magazine later exploded. (Anne S.K. Brown Military Collection, Brown University Library.)

Also powered by a foundry engine and built under the supervision of Commodore Matthew C. Perry, the USS *Mississippi* (1841), a 10-gun side-wheeler and sister ship to the USS *Missouri*, was one of the most widely traveled ships of her day. US Navy service took the *Mississippi* from the Mediterranean to the Far East, where she served as Perry's flagship in his opening of Japan in 1854. (PHM.)

A rare 1863 carte de visite shows the *Mississippi*, then part of the Union fleet under Rear Adm. David G. Farragut, on the Mississippi River. During the Siege of Port Hudson, Louisiana, she grounded near Confederate batteries, was set ablaze by her crew, then floated downriver and exploded. (Louisiana State University Libraries.*)

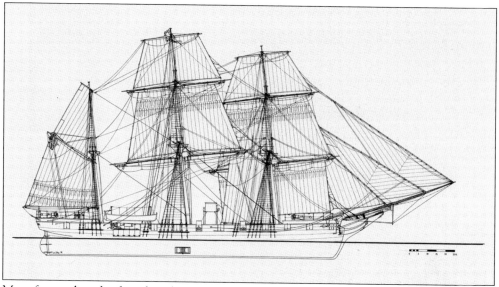

Manufactured at the foundry, the USS *Spencer* (1844), a revenue cutter, was the first iron-hulled ship made in the United States. The *Spencer* was fitted with the Hunter wheel system, an arrangement of paddles mounted horizontally and projecting through her sides below the waterline. Her service life lasted four years; she was converted to a lightship at the Willoughby's Spit station in Chesapeake Bay. (Dr. J.A. Tilley collection.)

Launched in 1855, the USS *Merrimac*, a steam frigate, was powered by WPF engines. During the evacuation of the Norfolk Navy Yard at the outbreak of the Civil War, the US Navy fired the ship, then out of service, to avoid Confederate capture. She burned to the waterline, sank, and was later raised and converted into the Confederate ironclad ram CSS *Virginia* (page 69). (Library of Congress.)

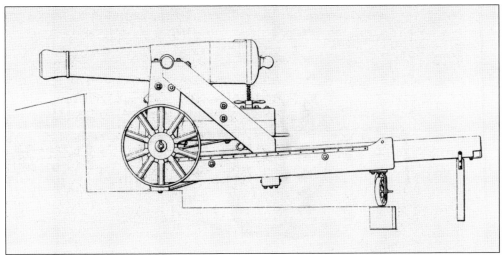

This diagram of a 32-pounder seacoast cannon on a Model 1839 front pintle barbette carriage is from *The Artillerist's Manual* (1860) by John Gibbons. The WPF's earliest contracts for ordnance came from the Army for coastal batteries and the Navy for warships. The foundry produced seacoast cannons and artillery pieces of other types and calibers—field and siege cannons, carronades, columbiads, howitzers, and mortars—in the pre–Civil War period. (PHM.)

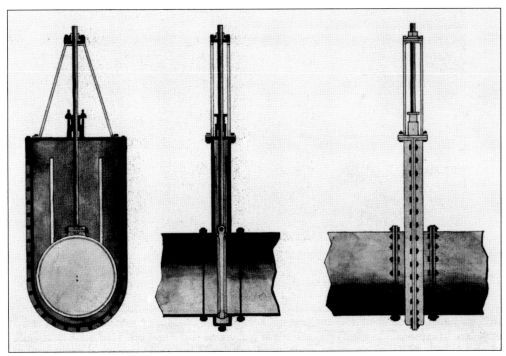

The WPF made pipes for the Croton Aqueduct, constructed between 1837 and 1842, to bring water 41 miles to New York City from the Croton River in New York State's Westchester County. At least one contract was awarded to the foundry in or about 1838. This illustration shows 36-inch water pipes and the placement of a stopcock for regulating or stopping the flow of water. (Library of Congress.)

In 1881, in the midst of a continuing drought, the flow of water from New York City's Central Park reservoir was temporarily but almost completely shut down. An illustration of the city's pipes, similar to or identical to those made by the foundry for the Croton Aqueduct system, with workers manning the stopcock, was published in the November 12, 1881, *Harper's Weekly* with an explanation of the water delivery system. (PHM.)

The foundry produced iron architectural components for the Edgar Laing Stores (1849), among other buildings. Designed by James Bogardus (1800–1874), a major figure in American iron architecture, the single unit consisted of three four-story warehouses wrapping a corner of Washington and Murray Streets in Lower Manhattan. It was the first building with a self-supporting cast-iron facade and included multiple elements, among them Doric-style engaged columns. (Library of Congress.)

The WPF made the condensing vertical-beam engine and pumps for the US Naval Dry Dock, completed in 1851 for the New York Navy Yard, later the Brooklyn Navy Yard. The side elevation of the machinery, with the cross and longitudinal sections of the well, is among 24 steel engravings in *The Naval Dry Docks of the United States* (1852) by Charles B. Stuart (1814–1881). He writes that the engine and pumps "in magnitude and power are not equaled in America" and that the Gothic frame was "finished in the most perfect manner." In 1848 and 1849, Stuart was New York State engineer and surveyor; he served in the Civil War as a Union army officer. The dock is now a landmark. (Ambrose Monell Library, Columbia University.)

This steam-driven beam engine and sugar mill (page 122) were produced for the Hacienda la Ezperanza, Manati, Puerto Rico, one of the most advanced sugar factories in Puerto Rico in the 1870s. The engine and its flywheel can be easily seen; the sugar mill (right) is visible through the spokes of the wheel. The mill had a life of 30 years and was not used after 1891. (Library of Congress.)

The sugar mill stands derelict, a rusting hulk, in this 1960s photograph. The words "West Point Foundry 1861" are partly visible on the machinery housing. The mill was designed to press cane juice from harvested sugarcane stalks. Countless stalks of sugarcane would have been fed through the mill's three rollers during the five-month harvest period from January through May. (Library of Congress.)

Two

THE MECHANICS
OF PRODUCTION
1860s

This photograph (dating after 1865) shows the general appearance of the WPF during the 1860s, its most productive period. The view is from Constitution Island, looking across the marsh of Foundry Cove to the dense complex of buildings. The foundry was in flux through the years as new buildings were erected and old ones torn down or used for new purposes. Details of this photograph appear on the following pages. (PHM.)

This section includes the molding shops (left) and smokestacks of the blast furnaces beyond. The spotting tower (center right, page 41) was used when testing cannons. Some products are seen on the ground: Parrott rifled cannons, Rodman cannons, and large pipes of a type used for aqueducts or other water systems (page 25). The stepped gable building is the machine shop. (PHM.)

In this closer view of the south side of the foundry grounds are the pattern shop (page 35) with a white surface and the office building with a cupola holding a bell. The wooded area in the distance is Garrison, adjacent to Cold Spring and also part of the town of Philipstown. During the late 1850s and 1860s, wealthy families from New York City were establishing summer estates there. (PHM.)

In this detail, five workers' houses, three of similar shape, straddle Rascal Hill. Among other locations where workers lived was Kemble Avenue, which linked Cold Spring's Main Street and the foundry and was its primary access road. Workers who lived in Nelsonville did not have far to come; the white Baptist church in the distance is in that village, just past the border with Cold Spring. (PHM.)

Harnessed oxen and a mule haul material or wait for loading; a flat railcar between what are probably raw materials rests on tracks used to carry products to other parts of the foundry complex, to the dock, and to long-distance trains. The gabled machine shop dominates the view despite the modest pre-1865 office building before it. The large buildings (left) are the molding shop complex. (PHM.)

A horse and wagon stand near the open door of the boiler shop tower. The vertical guy derrick, with its block and tackle system (back center), would have lifted and swung heavy objects, including cannons. Five triangular gun carriages are visible under the boom. Pipes are on the ground amid piles of debris, perhaps slag. (PHM.)

In this overview of the molding shop complex, which dates from the 1870s, the two tallest iron smokestacks vent cupola furnaces in which coke was mixed with iron to be melted for casting. The masonry chimney in front of the pair was that of the original gun foundry molding shop where cannons were cast throughout the Civil War. (PHM.)

The foundry operated around the clock during the Civil War, and workers like these, photographed between 1864 and 1866, put in 10-hour days. In March 1864, a general strike of some 1,200 workers shut down operations for two and a half days, reportedly because of inadequate wages. Workplace conditions may also have been a cause. Behind the workers are Parrott cannons and a large jib crane. (Yale University Art Gallery.)

The Gun Foundry (1864–66) by John Ferguson Weir (1841–1926), a rare American depiction of 19th-century industry, is a view of several WPF operations. It is painted in browns and glowing yellows and oranges. Weir grew up at West Point, where his father, the painter Robert Walter Weir, taught. Robert Parrott purchased this work; he stands directly behind Gouverneur Kemble (seated right) with others. (PHM.)

The painting's focal point is the casting process; molten iron is being poured from a casting ladle into a cannon mold during the casting of a Parrott rifled cannon for Civil War use. This strenuous, dangerous work exposed workers to intense heat. Two teams labor here, one at the ladle and pit, the other cranking gears to direct the ladle's movement, also controlled by the pulley operator. (PHM.)

In this detail, a Rodman cooling apparatus sits on top of a molding flask in a casting pit. The cooling apparatus introduced water into the bore to produce uniform contraction throughout a hollow-cast cannon. In an operation in the background, a worker stokes a furnace; its masonry chimney is to his left and can be seen from the outside in a photograph (page 32). (PHM.)

In this oil study by Weir, iron flows from a ladle into a mold. Two upright cannon flasks with ribbed framework stand next to a masonry chimney. Weir painted and drew many studies of gun foundry operations. In 1869, he became the first director of the newly organized Yale School of Fine Arts. He remained at Yale until 1913. (Yale University Art Gallery.)

Any iron object to be cast first needed a pattern, a replica made of wood and created in the foundry's pattern shop. This pattern would be used to produce the mold into which molten iron was poured during the casting process. The patternmakers pictured here were skilled carpenters who would handcraft the pattern to a slightly larger size that would allow for shrinkage when the iron cooled. (PHM.)

This stereoview image shows the interior of the machine shop where artillery pieces went through the final finishing process. On the furthest lathe, a 100-pounder Parrott rifle is undergoing the boring process to create the cannon tube. Rifling followed during which helical grooves were machined within the bore; rifling spins the projectile, giving it greater range and accuracy. The breech band and cannon exterior would also be machined. (PHM.)

Three massive jib cranes were centrally located in the boring shop for maximum utility. The rail tracks seen on the shop floor (left) were used to move cannons to and from the shop. The cranes lifted cannons, some weighing more than 26,000 pounds, from the railcars to machines and back. (PHM.)

A specialized piece of equipment (center right) gave cannon trunnions their final machining. Trunnions are protrusions from each side of the cannon that rest in the gun carriage; they provide the pivot point so that a cannon can be elevated to a desired trajectory. Cannons of various sizes undergoing final machining can be seen throughout the shop. (PHM.)

The pit lathe or wheel lathe allowed for the machining of large-diameter components such as iron wheels. The round faceplate was fitted with clamps that held the workpiece in place while it turned. The carriage on the right holds the cutting tools and was moved close to the rotating faceplate for machining the piece. (PHM.)

The back shot waterwheel seen here was the chief power source for the adjacent boring mill early in the foundry's existence. A wooden flume from a battery pond delivered water to the top of the wheel to drive it; water exited through a tailrace and was channeled back into Foundry Brook. The 36-foot-diameter wheel provided the power for the boring mill lathes. (PHM.)

A detail from *Atlas of New York and Vicinity* (1867) by F.W. Beers shows the foundry site and environs and part of its water supply system, composed of dams and reservoirs. The dam and waterfall closest to the site are indicated by a squared-off area below a bridge line (upper right). Water could be released from the system during a drought, enabling foundry work to continue. (PHM.)

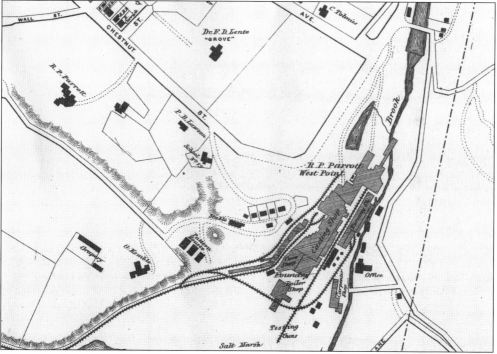

38

This 1890s photograph shows the waterfall of Foundry Brook, also known as Margaret's Brook, at the ridge of the foundry gorge. The dam itself was built with large blocks of stone, some of which remain (page 111). A sluice (lower left) directed water to the blowing engine of the original 1827 blast furnace. The brook's main flow (right) continued on a straighter course to Foundry Cove. (PHM.)

The foundry's vertical boring mill, seen here, is a large machine in which the workpiece is clamped to a movable table at bottom and is machined from above by a central, vertical boring tool. The foundry produced many engines and boilers, and the vertical boring mill would have played a substantial role in the manufacture of these products. (PHM.)

39

The partially covered hearth pit (foreground) and three large trip hammers can be seen in the blacksmith shop. To manufacture the breech band for the Parrott rifle, long bars of iron were heated in the hearth then coiled on a mandrel. The coil was reheated, placed in a cylinder, and hammered solid from the end, forming a wrought-iron band. Heated again, the band was fitted to the gun tube. (PHM.)

The machine shop, where a number of finishing operations occurred, had high-arched doorways so that large machine parts and other products could be loaded onto railcars. Railroad tracks ran through the doorways and into the building. Debris and discarded parts strewn about were typical. Neatness was not required, given the tight production schedules and also considering that materials might be reused. (PHM.)

Before 1865, the foundry's office buildings were small and architecturally less notable than this more formal one, constructed after the Civil War with profits from the wartime sale of ordnance. Commissioned by Parrott and built in 1865, it is the only building remaining on the foundry grounds. This photograph dates late in the century. (PHM.)

Several targets on Crow's Nest Mountain across the Hudson River were used to test, or prove, artillery pieces from this location at the edge of Foundry Cove. The booth at the top of the spotting tower provided a view of the targets from more than a mile away. The jib crane at right transferred the cannons from a rail system to the gun carriages at left for testing. (PHM.)

A row of Rodman smoothbore cannons is shown (left) along with several 200-pounder Parrott rifles in this image of the foundry's proving site. Test records indicate that a Parrott eight-inch 200-pounder rifle was fired from this location 100 times during the period of April 2 to May 19, 1862, to gauge the cannon's range and pressure. (PHM.)

Towards the end of the Civil War, attempts were made to improve the range and accuracy of smoothbore cannons by boring out the breech and inserting a rifled sleeve into the bore. Here, a modified 10-inch columbiad is seen on the WPF grounds following this conversion. The cannon could then be loaded from the breech rather than the muzzle. (Mark Forlow collection.)

A diagram from the August 28, 1862, *Harper's Weekly* shows Rodman's method of hollow casting heavy cannons. After casting, water was fed into the core to cool the cannon from the inside; up to 50,000 gallons of water were used to cool one cannon. By the end of the Civil War, this process was employed for the production of not only Rodman guns but also Parrott rifles. (Mark Forlow collection.)

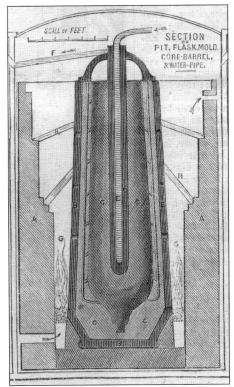

Robert Parrott owned blast furnaces that helped to supply the WPF with pig iron. The Greenwood Furnace (seen here in 1865) in Orange County, New York, was run by Peter Parrott, his brother. The furnace is the stone structure at center. Parrott also owned the Riddlesburg Furnace in Bedford County, Pennsylvania. (PHM.)

In *From the Earth to the Moon* (1865) by French novelist Jules Verne (1828–1905), the "manufactory of Goldspring" is contracted to transport to "Tampa Town" the "necessary materials for casting the cannon 'Columbiad'" for launching a projectile to the moon. Previously, "during the war," the manufactory "had furnished Parratt with the best cast-iron guns." This illustration is from an English translation (1873). (Rare Book & Manuscript Library, Columbia University.)

Three

WPF Ordnance
in Action during
the Civil War
1861 to 1865

A crew of the 1st Connecticut Artillery stands in firing position at a 20-pounder Parrott rifle. The artilleryman at left holds the sponge for cleaning the rifled bore once the round is fired. The crewman at right leans back ready to pull the lanyard on command. Upon firing, a friction primer is ignited, sending a flame down the vent to set off the charge in the bore. (Library of Congress.)

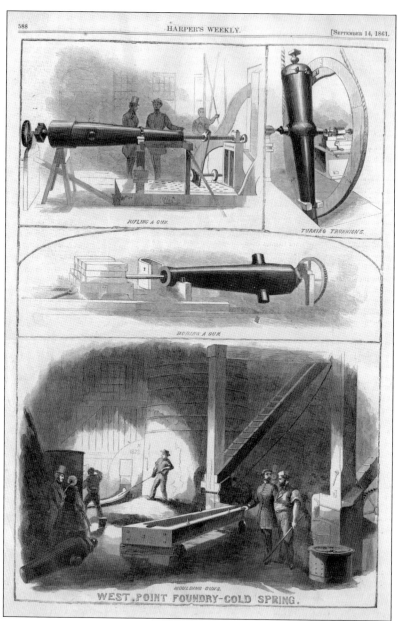

RIFLING A GUN.

TURNING TRUNNIONS.

BORING A GUN.

MOULDING GUNS.

WEST POINT FOUNDRY-COLD SPRING.

A well-known engraving detailing various operations of cannon making at the WPF was published in the September 14, 1861, *Harper's Weekly*, six months into the Civil War. Both smoothbore and rifled guns are pictured in the work, which illustrates the manufacture of both cannon types. A Parrott 20-pounder is undergoing the rifling process (top left); the panel next to it shows the turning of a smoothbore cannon trunnion on a large wheel. The center panel depicts the boring of what appears to be a smoothbore cannon. The bottom panel depicts the gun foundry, with a cannon mold, cranes, and furnaces during the casting process. A foundry worker is tapping molten iron from one of the two furnaces (dated 1823 in the image) behind the masonry chimney. Smoothbore cannons were manufactured at the foundry throughout the Civil War, but the new Parrott rifles dominated production time, with more than 2,900 of various calibers made during and immediately following the war. (Mark Forlow collection.)

The cover of *Leslie's Illustrated Weekly* for May 10, 1862, features this illustration of two 30-pounder Parrott rifles. The weapon was categorized as a siege cannon, being too heavy for roads and muddy fields. The cannon alone, without its carriage, weighed in excess of 4,000 pounds. First produced in 1861, the 30-pounder was the second type of Parrott rifled cannon manufactured, after the 10-pounders. (PHM.)

Men of Capt. Rufus D. Pettit's Battery B, 1st New York Light Artillery, are seen with their 10-pounder Parrott rifles at Fort Richardson in the vicinity of Fair Oaks, Virginia, during the Peninsula Campaign in the summer of 1862. The first rifle produced by Parrott, the 10-pounder, had two models—Model 1861 (2.9-inch bore) and Model 1863 (3-inch bore, which shared ammunition with the 3-inch ordnance rifle). (Library of Congress.)

On September 20, 1862, the day after the Battle of Antietam, near Sharpsburg, Maryland, men of the Pennsylvania Independent Battery E Light Artillery, under the command of Capt. Joseph M. Knap, are in formation with 20-pounder Parrott rifles. The first Civil War battle to occur on Union soil and the bloodiest in a single day in American warfare history, Antietam resulted in

a tactical standstill. This detail is from a picture taken by Alexander Gardner (1821–1882), one of the best-known photographers of the war. A staff photographer under Maj. Gen. George B. McClellan, the commander of the Army of the Potomac, Gardner developed his pictures of the Battle of Antietam in his transportable darkroom. Born in Scotland, he emigrated to the United States in 1856. (Library of Congress.)

Pres. Abraham Lincoln stands opposite Maj. Gen. George B. McClellan in October 1862 in the vicinity of the Battle of Antietam, in which Parrott rifles were the principal field artillery used. Lincoln had observed Parrott rifle testing at the WPF in June 1862 and been impressed by the accuracy and range of the 30-pounders at the Battle of Fort Pulaski near Savannah in April. (PHM.)

The Ringgold Battery, a light artillery detachment with 20-pounder Parrott cannons, drills in Pennsylvania, probably early in 1862. Capt. George W. Durell of Reading, Pennsylvania, is mounted (farthest right). The gun crews of six wear fatigue uniforms, appropriate for drill and battle. Water buckets, sponges, worms, and rammers are seen beneath the gun carriages. The location photographed has frequently been misidentified as Ringgold, Georgia. (Library of Congress.)

Harper's Weekly from August 8, 1863, shows the furious action at the Battle of Gettysburg, Pennsylvania, in early July. In this detail, a Parrott 20-pounder is seen askew in its battle-damaged gun carriage. The 20-pounder played a critical role at Gettysburg and other Civil War battlefields. The artistic source for this work is Alfred Waud (1828–1891), an artist correspondent known for his sketches for wood engravings for *Harper's*. (PHM.)

Mud-splashed 20-pounder Parrott rifles of the 1st New York Artillery are lined up at Fair Oaks, Virginia. The WPF produced two types of the ubiquitous 20-pounder—Model 1861 and Model 1863. The earlier version, seen here, had a muzzle swell. Parrott rifles, regardless of size, are easily distinguishable by the reinforced breech band at the rear of the cannon. (Library of Congress.)

Model 1840 eight-inch howitzers like this one, seen at the Battle of Seven Pines at Fair Oaks, were manufactured at the foundry as well as at other locations. Several surviving examples are stamped with the acronym *WPF* on the trunnion. The howitzer was designed to launch a shell at a high elevation of fire to achieve an airburst above and behind a fortified target. (Library of Congress.)

On the move near Richmond, Virginia, a train of 20-pounder Parrott rifles of the 1st New York Artillery readies for service. The cannon alone weighed about 1,800 pounds; with its carriage and limber, the entire kit weighed more than 4,400 pounds, putting it among the heaviest field weapons of the Civil War. Mobilizing the 20-pounder and limber required an eight-horse team. (Library of Congress.)

An illustration from the August 20, 1864, *Harper's Weekly* depicts the capture on July 27 of four 20-pounder Parrott cannons by the brigade of then colonel Nelson A. Miles, division of Brig. Gen. Francis C. Barlow, at the First Battle of Deep Bottom in Virginia. Parrott cannons were captured and recaptured throughout the war. The Confederacy manufactured rifled cannons based partly on Parrott's design. (PHM.)

A monument to "Independent Battery E, Pennsylvania Veteran volunteers, July 3rd 1863, 12th Army Corps" is seen in this post–Civil War photograph at the summit of Culp's Hill, Gettysburg, Pennsylvania. On that day, fire from Union Parrott rifles was so intense that a Confederate soldier called it "Artillery Hell." Three 20-pounder Parrott rifles with stacks of shells flank the monument. (Library of Congress.)

Surrounded by his staff, Maj. Gen. William Tecumseh Sherman leans on the breech band of a 20-pounder Parrott rifle positioned at a captured Confederate battery west of Atlanta. "A battery of field artillery is worth a thousand muskets," Sherman once said. This battery was renamed Federal Fort No. 7, one of several Union positions that formed a line of defense outside Atlanta in November 1864. (Special Collections, USMA Libraries.)

Officers and enlisted men pose in 1865 with a 100-pounder Parrott rifle at a neatly prepared Fort Totten garrison battery about three miles north of Washington, DC. The fort's only siege rifle, this Parrott provided support to nearby Fort Stevens during a Confederate attack in July 1864, proving Fort Totten to be a key position in the defense of the capital. (Library of Congress.)

Established on the James River near Richmond in October 1864, Fort Brady consisted of 10 gun emplacements garrisoned by the 1st Connecticut Artillery. A 100-pounder Parrot rifle is seen in a front pintle barbette carriage (foreground) with two 30-pounders in siege carriages and another 100-pounder beyond. These Parrott rifles frequently exchanged fire with Confederate forces on and across the river. (Library of Congress.)

During the Peninsula Campaign (1862), the Union organized siege preparations between the York and James Rivers that included 15 batteries with more than 70 heavy Parrott rifles. This Alexander Gardner photograph shows the 200-pounder rifle at Yorktown Battery No. 1, which also employed five 100-pounders. Manned by the 1st Connecticut Artillery, these cannons opposed Confederate forces across the York River. (Library of Congress.)

The Siege of Charleston Harbor (July 18–September 7, 1863) involved one of the most concentrated uses of heavy Parrott rifles during the Civil War. The objective was to clear the Confederate forts on Morris Island guarding the harbor entrance. Maj. Gen. Quincy Adams Gillmore is at his command post tent with staff. Shell and shot are scattered in the foreground, a 300-pounder flat-nosed bolt at right. (Library of Congress.)

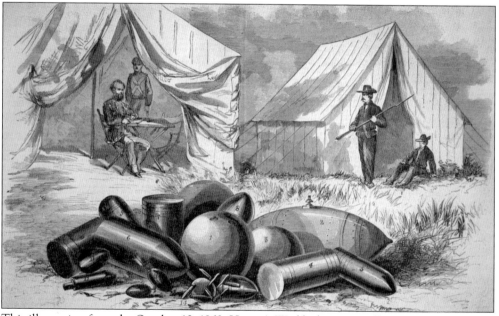

This illustration from the October 10, 1863, *Harper's Weekly* depicts a collection of ammunition types in front of Gillmore's tent. The pile includes Parrott shells for a 300-pounder (no. 6), 200-pounder (no. 8), and 100-pounder (no. 5). The foundry manufactured Parrott projectiles in all calibers for corresponding rifles and produced a range of projectile types as well—solid bolts, explosive shells, and incendiary shells. (PHM.)

This hand-drawn map of Charleston Harbor (September 1863) by Robert Sneden (1832–1918) shows Morris Island, Gillmore's camp, and Union artillery positions—the left breaching batteries and five parallels, or earthworks, extending up the Morris Island peninsula as far as the Confederate-held Fort Wagner. Also indicated on the map is the location of the Union's Swamp Angel battery in the marsh. It was established to fire exclusively on the city of Charleston. The disastrous failure of the July 18 infantry assault on Fort Wagner forced Gillmore to adopt siege tactics. An impressive store of Parrott heavy rifles was brought into position to shell Fort Wagner, Fort Gregg (also known as Battery Gregg, and renamed Fort Putnam in Union hands) at the tip of the peninsula, and Fort Sumter in the harbor (top). After nearly two months of bombardment by Union batteries, Morris Island was cleared of Confederate forces by September 7. (Library of Congress.)

A Haas & Peale photograph shows the Naval Battery at the center of the first parallel on Morris Island. Two massive 8-inch rifles, 200-pounders, are pictured, mounted on naval pivot carriages and manned by a Navy detachment from the USS *Wabash* under the command of Capt. Foxhall Parker. The Navy was known to provide additional siege artillery to the Army when required. (Library of Congress.)

Located to the right of the second parallel near the beach, Battery Brown, commanded by Capt. Charles Strahans of the 3rd Rhode Island Heavy Artillery, was armed with two 200-pounder Parrott rifles. One (left) has burst at the breech, throwing it forward and upending its gun carriage. A second burst cannon breech (lower left) has its elevating screw broken in pieces. (PHM.)

A dashing Capt. Jack J. Comstock Jr., Company M, 3rd Rhode Island Heavy Artillery, sits on the gun carriage base next to a burst 100-pounder Parrott rifle. Positioned to the left of the second parallel, Battery Rosecrans was armed with three of these siege weapons. One fired percussion shell while the other two fired solid shot. (PHM.)

Capt. Comstock stands amid scattered 100-pounder shells and their discarded boxes while the gun crews of Battery Rosecrans prepare their rifles for firing. The foundry produced 1.3 million projectiles during the Civil War. Two 100-pounders at this battery appear operational; a third gun carriage, barely visible, is missing its burst rifle. (Library of Congress.)

Gun crews of the 3rd Rhode Island Heavy Artillery ready a pair of 30-pounder Parrott rifles for firing on Fort Sumter. The left breaching batteries on Morris Island were positioned to shell and breach the masonry walls of the fort. Specially designed flat-nosed bolts were employed during the siege and proved extremely effective at penetrating masonry. (PHM.)

This 300-pounder Parrott rifle at Battery Strong, one of the left breaching batteries on Morris Island, burst at the muzzle when a shell exploded in the bore. The jagged muzzle was tooled down and the gun brought back into action. A second 300-pounder, positioned at Battery Chatfield, was later brought into play against Fort Sumter. It fired 1,007 rounds before meeting the same fate. (Library of Congress.)

The 300-pounder Parrott rifle above, viewed from the side, weighed more than 26,000 pounds and had the capacity to fire a shell 4,200 yards, far enough to reach Fort Sumter. The two 300-pounders at Morris Island saw more action in the Civil War than any of the other 40 guns of this type manufactured by the WPF. (PHM.)

After siege operations, the 200-pounder Parrott rifle in this Haas & Peale photograph lies dismounted behind its parapet at Battery Hays, one of the left breaching batteries oriented toward Fort Sumter (center) 4,172 yards away. A gun crew under the command of Capt. Robert G. Shaw of the 3rd Rhode Island Heavy Artillery bombarded the fort exclusively with solid shot (right) from this position. (Library of Congress.)

Two 100-pounder Parrott rifles overlook the marsh from their parapet at Battery Stevens, under the command of 1st Lt. James E. Wilson, 1st United States Artillery. Members of the gun crew stand on the parapet to view the action. A dismounted rifle rests amid empty barrels and stacks of projectile boxes. Battery Stevens was one of the left breaching batteries; its rifles—one throwing solid shot, the other percussion shells—bombarded Fort Wagner and Fort Sumter during the

Charleston Harbor siege operations. From August 17 to 23, the battery fired 566 projectiles (more than 46,000 pounds of WPF iron) at Fort Sumter, which was 4,278 yards away. During the bombardment of Fort Wagner on September 5 and 6, Battery Stevens fired 325 projectiles (more than 25,000 pounds of foundry iron). The bombproof shelter constructed inside the fort was reported to have withstood some 305 rounds. (Library of Congress.)

The Swamp Angel, perhaps the most famous cannon of the siege, if not the Civil War, was a 200-pounder Parrott rifle positioned in a specially constructed battery designed to support the weight of the gun in marsh conditions. The cannon fired on Charleston from four and a half miles away, its breech bursting on the 36th round, propelling it from its carriage up onto the parapet. (Library of Congress.)

At Battery Chatfield, adjacent to Fort Putnam, a Union gun crew prepares to fire a 200-pounder Parrott rifle. The cannon has no elevating screw. Normally found at the breech of the gun, this screw was turned in either direction to elevate or depress the tube. It has been replaced by a makeshift support of wooden blocks to achieve the elevation required to aim at Fort Sumter. (Library of Congress.)

Several Union soldiers stand near a 100-pounder Parrott rifle while others play cards (lower left) at a Fort Putnam battery on Morris Island. The shelling of Fort Sumter continued from this battery through September 1864 and reduced the fort walls to rubble, but Confederate forces held until February 1865. This photograph was taken near the end of the war. (Library of Congress.)

A 100-pounder Parrott rifle is seen at an extreme elevation at a Fort Putnam battery. The elevating screw is missing from the gun carriage. Parrott rifles were balanced at the trunnions and most commonly dropped at the breech end. This position is known as the cannon's preponderance. In rare cases when the rifle leaned forward, the cannon was said to have a negative or muzzle preponderance. (Library of Congress.)

Two 30-pounder Parrott rifles at rest in a Fort Putnam battery are surrounded by neatly stacked shells. Classified as a siege rifle, the 30-pounder could also be used as a sniping rifle. Both the Army and Navy appreciated its accuracy and rate of fire. Fort Sumter was less than 1,400 yards from this position, well within the range of these rifles. (Library of Congress.)

A variety of WPF-made products is stored at the Morris Island ordnance depot. At left are 30-pounder Parrott rifles in siege carriages. Wrought-iron chassis for front pintle barbette carriages occupy the foreground. (A barbette carriage allows a rifle an unrestricted line of fire over a parapet; a pintle is the iron pin that anchors a chassis.) Bolts and shells, loose and boxed, are stockpiled at right. (Library of Congress.)

A burst 100-pounder Parrott rifle lies on the beach at the Morris Island ordnance depot. Obstructions in the bore from beach sand as well as inadequate lubrication of shells were cited as reasons why rifles burst during the Charleston campaign. Manning these weapons could be a dangerous business; when they burst, injuries and deaths were a near certainty. (PHM.)

The USS *Monitor* is on the James River in July 1862 in this Civil War image. From the starboard side, the muzzle of one of two WPF-cast XI-inch Dahlgren smoothbore guns protrudes through the gun port of the turret. Four months earlier, the *Monitor* dueled the CSS *Virginia* at Hampton Roads in the first battle between ironclad warships. That action foreshadowed the ascendency of all-iron warships. (PHM.)

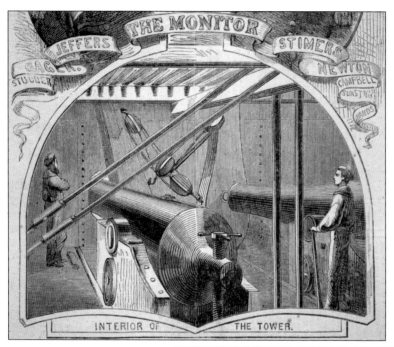

INTERIOR OF THE TOWER.

This engraving is from a two-page spread in the April 12, 1862, *Harper's Weekly* and is captioned "The 'Monitor' As She Is—Interior And Exterior." This section shows a rare glimpse of the interior of the *Monitor*'s turret, or tower, with her two massive foundry-made guns. The names of the *Monitor*'s crewmen appear on a pennant across the top. (PHM.)

Dahlgren guns were the most famous of the various types of artillery designed by Rear Adm. John A. Dahlgren (1809–1870), known as the "father of American naval ordnance." After promotion to captain in 1862, he became chief of the Navy's Bureau of Ordnance in Washington, DC. A rear admiral in 1863, he commanded the South Atlantic Blockading Squadron. This photograph is by Mathew Brady (1822–1896). (Library of Congress.)

The dramatic, inconclusive battle of the *Monitor* (foreground) and the CSS *Virginia* occurred on March 9, 1862, at the mouth of the James River, at the harbor Hampton Roads, Virginia. The *Virginia* was created from the hull of the *Merrimac* (page 24), a steam frigate with a WPF engine. She was armored with iron plating above her wooden hull. This contemporaneous lithograph is by Henry Bill (1824–1891). (Library of Congress.)

Surrounded by crew members, a 100-pounder Parrott rifle mounted in a naval pivot carriage is seen on board the USS *Mendota*, a side-wheel gunboat launched in January 1863. Armed with two 100-pounders, the *Mendota* served the Navy both as a bombardment gunboat and a picket ship preventing Confederate trade with foreign countries. The 100-pounder became a favorite of the Navy, along with the 200-pounder. (PHM.)

On the *Mendota,* a 100-pounder nestles in a pivot carriage and slide, its breech and elevating screw in full view. The US Navy ordered more than 1,200, nearly half of all Parrott rifles made at the foundry. Navy gun crews maintained these weapons with great care; they were thoroughly cleaned and the shells properly lubricated. By the war's end in 1865, only 19 of the 352 Navy 100-pounders had burst. (Library of Congress.)

Sunday Morning Inspection on Board the Gun-Boat 'Metacomet' in the December 10, 1864, *Harper's Weekly* pictures a Parrott 100-pounder. The wooden side-wheel steamer, named after a Wampanoag war chief, functioned as a gunboat in Adm. David G. Farragut's West Gulf Blockading Squadron and in August helped to capture the ironclad ram CSS *Tennessee,* a major threat to the Union blockade of Mobile Bay. (PHM.)

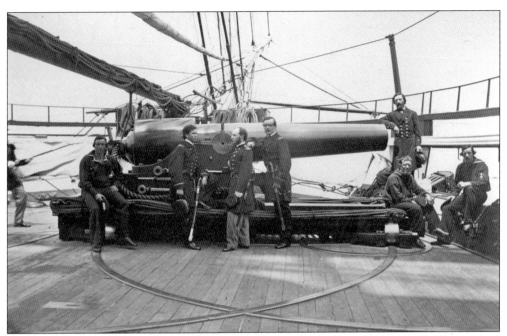

Officers of the USS *Wabash* pose near their forward pivot gun, a 150-pounder naval rifle. Terminology differed between the Army and Navy in describing the 8-inch Parrott rifle. The Army called it a 200-pounder; the Navy referred to it as a 150-pounder. The difference related to the projectile size; the Navy employed a shorter round that weighed less. (US Army Heritage and Education Center.)

This July 18, 1863, *Harper's Weekly* cover image depicts the bombardment of Port Hudson, Louisiana. Aboard the USS *Richmond*, sailors work a 100-pounder Parrott cannon about two miles below Confederate batteries, which extended three miles along the east bank of the Mississippi River. The illustration's commentary notes that the projectiles easily reached the batteries' center. The lettering on the ammunition box (bottom right) refers to the 100-pound projectile. (PHM.)

The Pet Parrott on the United States Steamer 'Richmond' in a Storm, an illustration from the May 14, 1864, *Harper's Weekly*, depicts the same 100-pounder Parrott cannon (page 71) breaking loose in high seas off Mobile, Alabama. Notes accompanying the image indicate that sailors tried to rescue the cannon while not putting themselves "in too close proximity to the frolicsome Parrott." The *Richmond* was a wooden steam sloop. (PHM.)

Bursting of the 100-Pound-Parrott Gun on Board the United States Steamer 'Juniata,' December 24, 1864, in the January 21, 1865, *Harper's Weekly*, illustrates an event no photographer of the day could have recorded. During a live engagement at Fort Fisher, North Carolina, the *Juniata*'s only 100-pounder rifle burst violently, killing five sailors and wounding eight others. (PHM.)

This Civil War–era stereoview image shows two Parrott rifles—a 100-pounder and a 200-pounder—at West Point's seacoast battery among foundry-made smoothbore cannons produced before the war. The mast of a sloop at West Point's north dock is visible beyond them. Cadets received artillery training at this site; their cannons aimed at targets at the base of Crow's Nest Mountain. (Mark Forlow collection.)

A 100-pounder Parrott rifle mounted on a front pintle carriage is pictured at West Point's seacoast battery on the north side of the academy's grounds. Developed in the autumn of 1861, the gun was a larger version of the field rifles manufactured at the foundry in the previous year. Classified as a seacoast and naval rifle, it saw use in siege operations as well. (Mark Forlow collection.)

The foundry cast many Rodman cannons like this 10-inch smoothbore mounted on a center pintle carriage at West Point's seacoast battery. A hoist at the front of the carriage facilitated the loading of the cannon's 125-pound shot. The Rodman had a distinctive bottle shape and used a ratchet system at the back of the gun to elevate it for the desired range. (Mark Forlow collection.)

Thomas Jackson Rodman (1816–1871), an inventor, ordnance specialist, and career Army officer, made many improvements to Union artillery. He designed the Rodman cannon, cast at the WPF and elsewhere for use during the Civil War, and was awarded the rank of brevet brigadier general for his Civil War service. This portrait of him appears with an article on his cannon in the November 19, 1864, *Harper's Weekly*. (PHM.)

Four 30-pounder Parrott rifles are positioned behind the prepared earthworks of West Point's siege battery in this Civil War–era picture. Buildings of the academy's ordnance laboratory are in the distance. The 30-pounder required a crew of nine. As at the seacoast battery (page 73) at the river's edge, cadets received artillery training firing at the target area at the base of Crow's Nest Mountain. (Mark Forlow collection.)

At West Point's Knox Battery, a 100-pounder (front) and a 200-pounder Parrott rifle flank a Rodman gun. The view is east across the Hudson River; the guns point downriver. A Colonial-period emplacement, this battery served no practical purpose when this photograph was taken in the early 1900s. By then, the cannons were for display only. (Mark Forlow collection.)

A couple poses next to 20-pounder Parrott rifles at Little Round Top. From this position, the second-highest point at Gettysburg, rifle rounds reached Picket's advance to Union lines on Cemetery Ridge more than a mile away—with devastating effect. The 44th New York Volunteer Infantry Regiment monument (1893) is in the background. (Library of Congress.)

The statue of Maj. Gen. Gouverneur Kemble Warren (1830–1882) at Gettysburg was erected in 1888 in honor of his last-minute defense of Little Round Top, which included the effective use of Parrott rifles. An 1850 West Point graduate born in Cold Spring, Warren was named after Gouverneur Kemble (page 14), who was a friend of his father. This photograph dates about 1903. (PHM.)

Four

INTO THE COMMUNITY
1830s TO 1890s

Gouverneur Kemble, the WPF's driving force, asked budding architect Thomas Wharton (page 17) to create a chapel for Catholic foundry workers. Designed with Kemble's help, the resulting Chapel of Our Lady (1834) is in the Tuscan style and faces the Hudson near Foundry Cove. This engraving by Joseph A. Adams (1803–1880), after a work by Robert W. Weir (1803–1889), was published in the November 8, 1834, *New-York Mirror*. (PHM.)

Vibration shocks caused by the testing of Parrott cannons during the Civil War damaged the chapel. Beginning about 1867, it was enlarged, renovated in the Victorian style, and renamed St. Mary's. Robert Parrott, the superintendent of the foundry until 1867, provided funds for the project. The building was later restored close to its original appearance and is now called the Chapel of Our Lady Restoration (pages 77, 126). (Mark Forlow collection.)

In 1830, the WPF built a school on the ridge nearby. Originally for apprentices, including many Irish immigrants, it also served workers' children. From 1867 to 1891, it was part of the local school system. Purchased by the Putnam County Historical Society in 1960, the building, now the home of the Putnam History Museum, has been enlarged, renovated, and partly restored. (PHM.)

In this Currier & Ives lithograph (1862), two men converse along the ridge above the foundry. The road below them was one approach to the foundry from the village. The artist, Frances Flora Palmer (1812–1876), drew more than 200 scenes for Currier & Ives, many unsigned. (PHM.)

Parrott donated land and funds to build St. Mary-in-the-Highlands (1868), designed by George Edward Harney (1840–1924). It is said to have been his gift to the community in celebration of the end of the Civil War. The building is primarily granite, quarried from the Cold Spring estate of financier Frederick James. Parrott's carriage house is in the distance; it is now used commercially. (St. Mary-in-the-Highlands Archive.)

Gouverneur Kemble, a bachelor, hosted many gatherings for friends and acquaintances in military and literary spheres, including Salmagundi Club members. In the 1860s, he stands on the porch of his home (page 38), Marshmoor, in front of the seated Bvt. Lt. Gen. Winfield Scott, who would die in 1866. Robert Parrott is at the far left; Kemble's brother William, center, wears a hat; Alonso Alden (a lieutenant colonel in 1864) faces him, in uniform. (PHM.)

Parrott's residence stood on higher ground between the foundry's school and St. Mary-in-the-Highlands with a view of the river. He owned many houses in Cold Spring. This lithograph was based on a drawing by British immigrant Edwin Whitefield (1816–1892), best known for views of North American cities and New England Colonial houses. (PHM.)

Mary (née Kemble) Parrott (1799–1890) sits in her carriage outside her home, which is no longer standing. The Parrotts, who were childless, married in 1839 when Mary was 40 and Parrott 35. Mary and her brothers Gouverneur and William were among six children of Peter Kemble and Gertrude Gouverneur. Peter and brothers of his wife owned the commercial house of Gouverneur & Kemble in New York City. (PHM.)

A *Pic-Nic on the Hudson* (1863) by Thomas P. Rossiter (1817–1871) depicts Gouverneur Kemble (seated, far right) and Robert and Mary Parrott (behind him) with prominent friends from the Highlands, including publisher and poet George Pope Morris (center) and Robert W. Weir (left, on boulder), painter and professor at West Point. Rossiter (bearded, left rear) had a home in Cold Spring. (Julia L. Butterfield Memorial Library.)

As Gouverneur Kemble had previously done, Robert Parrott took a paternalistic role in providing homes for foundry workers on land owned by him or the WPF. These houses along Parrott Street in Cold Spring are among 10 built in the 1860s and are typical of single-family homes of the period. Providing housing for workers with families was expected to discourage turnover in the workforce. (Photograph by Mark Forlow.)

In the 1890s, foundry workers pose during wintertime on a bridge that crossed Foundry Brook, just upstream from the dam and waterfall at the top of the foundry gorge. Some workers and their families lived in this area on what was called Vinegar Hill, on the south side of the brook (left). The area took its name from the Battle of Vinegar Hill in the Irish Rebellion of 1798. (PHM.)

Local photographs from the late 19th century reveal that foundry workers sometimes made small iron cannons that children were allowed to play with, including on patriotic days. Cannons like this one were not necessarily toys; they were probably signal cannons, which were heavy and would not have been easily pulled. (PHM.)

Kemble, a friend of important military men, established a militia called the Kemble Guard in 1847 during the Mexican War (1846–48). The guard was part of the 6th Company, 18th Regiment, and 7th Brigade of New York State. It saw no action in the Civil War and was mustered out in 1863. Later, these local youths called their militia-like organization by the same name. (PHM.)

Gouverneur Kemble organized a band, which played on patriotic and other occasions. Photographs show the group changing membership over the years. In this undated example, the band sits in front of the town hall of Philipstown, which was built in 1867 and still serves Cold Spring and other parts of the town. (PHM.)

Because most foundry workmen lived in Cold Spring and adjacent Nelsonville (part of Philipstown), it was natural that the love of baseball that developed in those villages in the latter decades of the 19th century would spawn a WPF team. Many teams were formed and were often sponsored by local businesses. (PHM.)

Five

Post–Civil War Period with New Ownerships and New Products
1866 to 1911

In 1866, the foundry made the many iron components of the second lighthouse (foreground) built at Cape Canaveral, a sandy hook about midway along Florida's Atlantic coast. An earlier structure, the North Light (shown partly dismantled), was constructed by another company in 1829. Spiral or horizontal stripes on lighthouses give greater visibility and distinguish one from another. (The State Archives of Florida.)

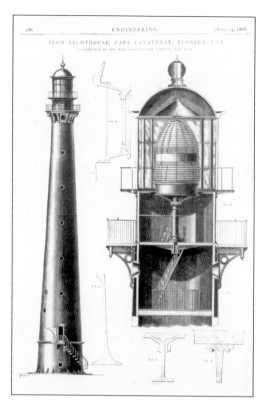

IRON LIGHTHOUSE, CAPE CANAVERAL, FLORIDA, U.S.A.

CONSTRUCTED BY THE WEST POINT FOUNDRY COMPANY, NEW YORK.

This illustration from the September 14, 1866, *Engineering* magazine depicts the iron plating of the basic structure and the iron stairway and landings of the Cape Canaveral Lighthouse. The foundry did not manufacture its lens or lamp. Many lighthouses with iron components and masonry or brick exteriors were built along the Atlantic and Gulf coasts in the 19th century. Because of cliff erosion, this lighthouse was moved and relit. (PHM.)

Iron inner elements of the Block Island Southeast Light, built in 1875, were also made at the WPF. Block Island lies 13 miles off the Rhode Island coast. The lighthouse was built on Mohegan Bluffs and is not as tall as some lighthouses because of the elevation of the bluffs. Deactivated in 1900, it became a National Historic Landmark in 1997. (Library of Congress.)

This view of the Southeast Light shows the base of its ornate interior spiral staircase, which leads to the lantern. The iron castings of its newels, railings, stair treads, and risers are visible. The light was moved about 100 yards from its original location when cliff erosion endangered its stability. (Library of Congress.)

This underside view of the watch room floor, beneath the lantern, includes the iron castings for the stairway, floor support beams, and floor panels. Iron was also used for two outer walkways and railings, seen in the exterior view opposite. This photograph and the one at top are from a US government survey, the Historic American Engineering Record. (Library of Congress.)

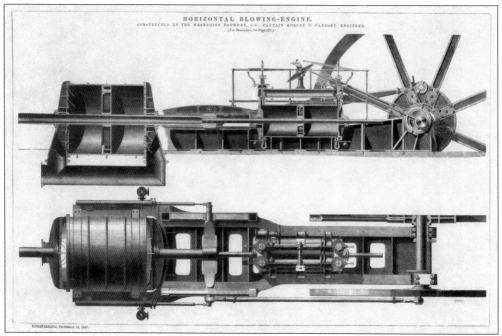

This detailed engraving from the September 13, 1867, *Engineering* magazine features Robert Parrott's design of a new version of the horizontal blowing engine, which had been built numerous times before in various sizes. Two of the largest engines of this design were made for the blast machines of smelting furnaces operated by Messrs. H. Burden and Sons, Troy, New York, and Chestnut Hill Furnaces, Columbia, Pennsylvania. (PHM.)

Weir's *Forging the Shaft* (1874–77), like his *The Gun Foundry* (1864–66; page 33), is notable in treating American industrial history. It shows the forging of a large propeller shaft for an ocean liner, one type of ship that replaced paddle-driven ones in transatlantic voyages. This is the second version of the work; the first, painted in 1868, was destroyed by fire in 1869. (The Metropolitan Museum of Art.)

Although the foundry did significantly less business in cannons and projectiles following the Civil War, there was occasional demand from foreign nations for ordnance. In this illustration, *Spanish Gunboat—Testing Her Guns at Cold Spring, on the Hudson,* from the October 16, 1869, *Harper's Weekly,* the ship's bow carries what appears to be a large gun, probably a Parrott 100-pounder, a preferred weapon of the US Navy. (PHM.)

Iron production levels fell after the Civil War. During the 1870s and 1880s, efforts were made to revive the foundry, restructured as Paulding, Kemble & Company as of 1870 and run by Gouverneur Kemble's nephews— Gouverneur Paulding (1829–1913; at right), James N. Paulding, Peter Kemble, and Gouverneur Kemble Jr. (an honorific). At his death in 1877, Parrott had left them his interests in the property. (PHM.)

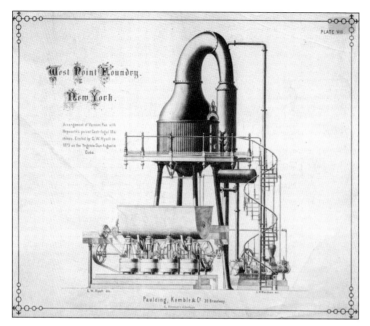

The foundry built this eccentric-looking arrangement of machines in 1873 for a sugar refinery at San Augustin, Cuba. The vacuum pan, a tank located at the top of the machinery, facilitated rapid evaporation and condensation of cane juice, boiling at a low temperature during the production of sugar syrup. A centrifugal machine (bottom), patented by S.S. Hepworth, separated fluids from the raw product through rotating action. (PHM.)

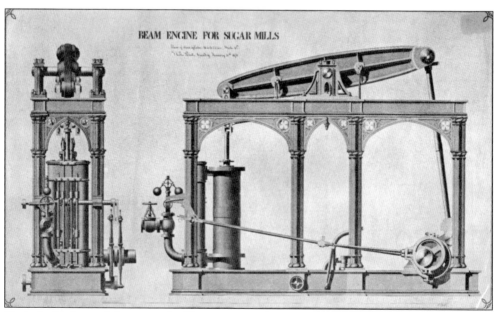

Typical of industrial design in the Victorian period, ornate cast-iron columns and vaulting are incorporated into the superstructure of this plan of a steam-powered beam engine manufactured by the WPF for sugar mills. Dated January 30, 1878, this Paulding, Kemble & Co. illustration indicates that the engine could be built with cylinders of a diameter of 18 inches to 24 inches with a four-foot stroke. (PHM.)

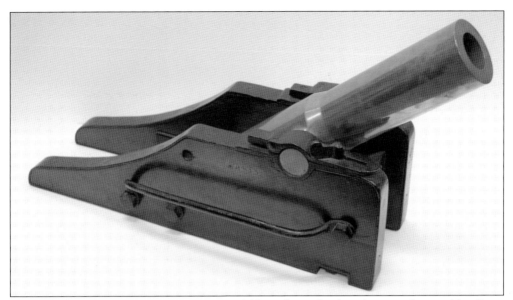

This Lyle line-throwing gun, among some 200 made at the foundry, was designed by Capt. David A. Lyle, a West Point and MIT graduate, after the US Life-Saving Service requested such a gun from the Army in 1877. Of three sizes, in bronze, the 2.5-inch bore, shown here, became the standard. The gun was mainly used to assist those in distress offshore. (West Point Museum Collection, USMA.)

Foundrymen pose for this group portrait outside the machine shop in the latter part of the century. The 1860 Census shows about 480 WPF workers, many of them Irish immigrants. That number nearly tripled during the Civil War and declined after it. Daily ledgers recording workers' names, types of work, hours, and wages are now historical items. (PHM.)

Office employees stand in front of the 1865 office building. Those who worked here included drafting engineers and employees who handled orders as well as at least one inspector of ordnance, Albert L. Terwilliger, who was also a local photographer. No photographs of Robert Parrott or other leading WPF figures taken on the property are known to the authors. (PHM.)

A pneumatic dynamite gun, designed by Edmund Zalinski (1849–1909), points northward up the Hudson River from the foundry's dock. Several investors set up the Pneumatic Dynamite Gun Company, New York, and contracted the WPF to manufacture Zalinski's gun. Production of the guns occurred in 1893, although few were made. This unusual coastal and naval artillery piece used compressed air to deliver a large dynamite charge up to four miles. (PHM.)

Beginning in 1894, the Army purchased several dynamite guns for use in coastal batteries, but service life was short as all were decommissioned in 1904. The gun succeeded in delivering a high explosive charge on target, but the ancillary equipment needed to operate the gun—the steam boiler and compressor—proved too impractical for success. (PHM.)

In 1898, the J.B. & J.M. Cornell Co., then run by the Cornell brothers John Milton and Henry Meigs, took over the foundry. Their father, John Black Cornell (1821–1887), pictured here, had been a major force at Cornell for many years. In 1856, his patent for a metallic surface for fireproof partitions supporting plaster contributed to the construction of fireproof high-rise buildings. (Cornell Iron Works Archives.)

John Black Cornell (page 93) and his son John Milton (1846–1934) established the J.B. & J.M. Cornell Co. in 1870. By 1880, it had become one of the largest manufacturers in New York City and by 1898 had produced iron and steel for major projects. As of 1898, the Cornell office building with an adjacent riveting shop was at Twenty-sixth Street and Eleventh Avenue. (PHM.)

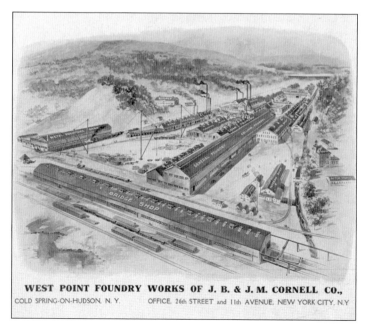

WEST POINT FOUNDRY WORKS OF J. B. & J. M. CORNELL CO.,
COLD SPRING-ON-HUDSON, N. Y.   OFFICE, 26th STREET and 11th AVENUE, NEW YORK CITY, N.Y.

This illustration, from about 1905, shows the expansion of the foundry during the Cornell period. New buildings included the column foundry and metal furniture and bridge shops; the machine shop and pattern shops were enlarged. The bridge shop produced at least one bridge, the Niagara Street Bridge in Tonawanda, New York. An earlier Cornell partnership had made the Bow Bridge (1862), designed by Calvert Vaux for New York's Central Park. (PHM.)

Dating about 1900, this photograph shows the extensive complex of tightly clustered buildings and smokestacks that made up the Cornell foundry. The narrow gorge, steep hillsides, and nearby Foundry Cove prevented wider expansion of the foundry operations. A rare postcard of this view exists, the only one known to depict the foundry. (PHM.)

A foundry worker stands next to a guy derrick, a unique crane consisting of a mast that rotated at the base; it was fixed in place by supporting guy wires at the top. A boom is hinged at the base of the mast with its extended end reeved to the top of the mast by an arrangement of pulleys to allow the raising and lowering of a load. (PHM.)

The column finishing shop (left) is seen here with the bridge shop in the distance. A guy derrick is moving a heavy casting into place. A large quantity of structural columns is stacked for shipping. By this period, the foundry had several guy derricks that were operated by electric motors. (PHM.)

By far the largest addition to the Cornell operations was the column shop complex. Included within this immense ironclad structure were a general foundry, a column and finishing shop, and a loam shop. A small locomotive facilitated the moving of material and finished products to and from the building complex. The foundry could produce up to 200 tons of castings per day. (PHM.)

These workers are pictured with a small steam engine, part of the foundry's internal railway system, which took material to carriers on long-distance tracks or to the foundry's dock. Named the *Pioneer*, the engine was originally designed to pull trains on elevated tracks in New York City. It was featured alone on a postcard published by a local Cold Spring druggist. (PHM.)

A series of staircases descend to the foundry from the top of the ravine, providing access for workers. Two charging bridges used for conveying materials are visible; one (left) has rails for transporting coke and iron from the railway siding to the central cupola furnaces in the molding house. The second bridge (right) terminated near a separate furnace in the same shop. (PHM.)

Seen through an open window, a metal tubular flume, sometimes called a penstock, descends from a battery pond (for storing water) to a water turbine in the foreground. As late as 1893, the foundry used the back shot waterwheel as a source for power. By the Cornell period, a water turbine and electric motors were used to power machines in foundry buildings. (PHM.)

Workers pose on and around the molding equipment in the foundry's column shop. Overhead is a traveling crane designed by the Cornell company; it spans the room and rides elevated tracks that run along both sides of the shop walls. This crane was electric and capable of supporting great loads. Columns and other heavy castings were moved to railcars using this ingenious machine. Skylights and windows provide light. (PHM.)

This Cornell photograph shows a long interior view of the column shop. Two core ovens (right) were for drying molds before casting. To the immediate right is an open-sided molding room for the production of smaller pieces; it contained several additional core ovens. Both rooms had dirt floors and substantial doorways to allow for railcar entry. (PHM.)

Three core ovens with their doors open can be seen at the rear of the small molding room next to the column shop. Wheeled tables for transporting the prepared molds for drying ride tracks into the ovens. Jib cranes throughout the room move the molds to and from the tables. Molding core boxes—some empty, some in use—are scattered across the shop floor. (PHM.)

A large, skeletal, wooden pattern dominates the loam shop, with many foundry workers assembled nearby. The material used to create a casting mold was loam, a mixture of sand and clay. Once the mold was formed, the pattern was removed, leaving a void in the mold to accept the molten iron. (PHM.)

The top of a molding flask and hoist ring (foreground) are visible in one of the many casting pits in the molding shop. Two cupola furnaces occupy the center right. Four jib cranes are located centrally through the length of the shop, which produced the foundry's heavy castings. (PHM.)

In the Cornell period, an additional side room (left) was added to the pattern shop to accommodate longer workbenches. Wooden patterns for columns and machine parts to be cast are in progress throughout the shop. The decorative eagle that overlooked the room from the corner at an earlier time now occupies a central position (page 35). (PHM.)

The foundry machine shop expanded after the Civil War, nearly tripling in size by 1887. Included in the shop inventory were 11 lathes, 16 planers, 5 shapers, 3 hydraulic presses, 6 drill presses, 3 boring machines, and 7 jib cranes for lifting heavy castings to and from the machines. During Cornell ownership, at least three electric motors powered the line shafts for the machines. (PHM.)

Machinists and young apprentices sit and stand amid machines and behind two large, circular workpieces. Other machine parts are packed in open-sided wooden crates (right) for transport. This room in the machine shop was transformed many times over the years; here, it contains a machine driven by a large belt crossing the room diagonally and a coal-burning stove and flue. (PHM.)

A metal lathe made by the Lucius W. Pond tool company of Worchester, Massachusetts, is shown in the foundry's machine shop holding a nearly finished translating roller, used in the breech assembly of the Model 1888 breech-loading rifle (B.L.R.). Calipers and other machine tools, as well as a machinist's jacket, hang on the wall. The machine shop also had larger lathes with the capacity to handle heavier projects. (PHM.)

A gun section for a Model 1888 ten-inch B.L.R. stands erect and rests on large wooden blocks in the machine shop. A crude wooden scaffold has been arranged to allow workers access to water pipes and hoist points at the top of the gun section. At the bottom, jets of water from a hose are directed around the outside of the component to cool it for the fitting of an exterior band. It is also cooled from the inside by water from pipes descending through the top; water drains from the building through an opening in the floor. This fine photograph and the two following are from glass-plate negatives from an extensive collection at the Putnam History Museum. They were probably taken by Albert L. Terwilliger (1875–1948), director of ordnance at the foundry at the beginning of the 20th century and a serious local photographer who also photographed operations at the West Point Foundry. Terwilliger grew up in nearby Nelsonville. (PHM.)

An apparatus directs jets of water onto the trunnion band of a Model 1888 ten-inch B.L.R. to cool it for fitting. This gun was made entirely of steel and when assembled weighed 30 tons. Its components would probably not have been made at the foundry but would have been supplied from other sources, with the foundry providing only final assembly and machining. The 10-inch gun was used in concert with the Model 1896 New Howell disappearing gun carriage, also assembled at the WPF. The setting is one of the rooms of the enlarged machine shop complex. Block and tackle pulleys hang from above; large machine lathes can be seen in the next room. (PHM.)

A Model 1888 ten-inch B.L.R. awaits machining and assembly in the machine shop with two other guns in view behind. An interrupted-screw breechblock (foreground, right) and a trunnion band farther back (far right) are on the workbenches. An 1871 patented Thorne portable drilling machine (center) can be moved to a workpiece and is driven by a rope that extends to a line shaft high on the wall. (PHM.)

Under Cornell ownership, the foundry continued to manufacture not only artillery but also gun carriages and projectiles. A New Howell disappearing carriage and a Model 1888 ten-inch B.L.R., weighing 33 tons, are being assembled in the foundry's machine shop. Designed for coastal service, the gun carriage, shown in the firing position, would drop the gun down behind a parapet after firing for reloading and concealment from enemy warships. (PHM.)

Built about 1905, the ironclad metal furniture shop provided the facilities for fabricating and finishing furniture. General metal and machine work were done in the main section of the building. Other rooms were devoted to finishing—dipping and japanning to produce a lacquered finish. Five japan ovens were on hand for drying the finished work. (PHM.)

This cylinder block for a Corliss steam engine stands by the foundry's weigh station (right), ready for shipment to Robert Wetherell & Company in Chester, Pennsylvania. The company specialized in boilers and originated a new design for the Corliss engines, many of which were large. Notes on the back of this photograph indicate that the block weighed 23 tons. (PHM.)

Two large, bowl-shaped castings are seen on board a flatbed railcar pulled by a foundry locomotive from the weigh station. A worker strikes a pose between the two objects. The weight of the castings is inscribed on the side of each, with 22,000 pounds indicated at left and 21,800 at right. (PHM.)

In the foundry's latter years, as in its early ones, some products were transported to Hudson River ports either for delivery or for further work such as assembly and fitting. Notes on the back of this photograph cite this location as South Amboy, New Jersey. The products on the barge are huge pipe sections, their size emphasized by the presence of a woman standing inside one of them. (PHM.)

Six

DETERIORATION, ARCHAEOLOGY, AND PRESERVATION
1912 TO 2013

Cornell ceased production in 1909 and finally closed in 1911. Buildings began deteriorating or were dismantled, although over the years other companies ran their operations in some of them. Buildings of the machine shop complex are to the left; the large building on the right side of Foundry Brook was for pattern storage. (PHM.)

Two men perch atop the twisted skeleton of one of the foundry's long buildings. The mast and boom of a guy derrick are visible, as are abandoned machinery and materials within the building's framework. Many of the foundry's buildings had been reduced to heaps of scrap by the 1930s. (PHM.)

In 1924, Louis Mayer (1869–1969) did a series of 15 large charcoal drawings of the abandoned foundry and houses and streets of Cold Spring. He had a studio on the village's Main Street in the 1920s. His depictions of the foundry ruins are untitled; however, this cavernous interior is probably one of the machine shops (page 40), which had large arched doorways. (PHM.)

These women clasp arms like friendly coworkers near the former metal furniture shop, built about 1905 (page 107). Their dresses date the photograph at about 1920. The women would have worked for one of several companies that used foundry buildings in the 1920s and/or 1930s, including the Astoria Silk Works and a pearl button factory. (Josephine Doherty collection.)

The steel bridge now serving Route 9D was built almost directly over the remains of the dam at the edge of the foundry gorge (page 39). The footings of the old bridge, which crossed about 50 feet upstream, are visible amid the trees (center), as is the stone retaining wall for an access road that ran down the gorge into the foundry complex. (Photograph by Jan Thacher.)

This ruin near the dam seen on the previous page is among the oldest on the foundry site and was part of the original 40-foot-tall blast furnace (page 14). The furnace provided continuing smelting operations until 1844 when it became more cost-effective to procure quality pig iron from other sources. The arch is made of bricks, which were often scavenged from around the foundry site. (PHM.)

The original gun foundry building appears in ruins in this 1970s photograph. The structure had a masonry chimney and housed the foundry's main air furnace. When artillery contracts declined in the 1870s, this building was abandoned. One of two cast-iron smokestacks for the once adjacent cupola furnaces lies in pieces (foreground). (PHM.)

Only the foundry's office building (1865) survived; it was put to use by various businesses until finally abandoned. This photograph dates from the 1970s, when archaeologist Edward S. Rutsch and associates investigated the foundry site. The team, which included project director Ralph Brill (then a resident of Cold Spring), produced a large, informative report in 1979, mainly on archaeological diggings and the history of the foundry complex. (Photograph by Michael Spozarsky; PHM.)

In two phases between 1989 and 1993, archaeologist Joel W. Grossman and associates excavated areas of the foundry site to better understand and thus prevent any disturbance to its historical aspects before any large-scale excavation took place. The work went on prior to and in conjunction with the cleanup of the former battery plant nearby and the marsh at Foundry Cove by the US Environmental Protection Agency beginning in 1989. (USEPA.)

Near Foundry Cove, Joel Grossman's team members, wearing protective clothing, unearth the foundry's center pintle gun platform. This stationary fixture allowed the gun carriage to pivot for aiming when proving Parrott siege rifles and other heavy artillery types during the Civil War. The platform can be seen on the cover of this book supporting a massive 300-pounder Parrott cannon. (USEPA.)

A Grossman team member works with the beams of a once powerful jib crane, one of the largest among thousands of artifacts and shards uncovered. The crane (pages 41, 42) was used throughout the Civil War; it stood near the spotting tower and could lift a 300-pounder cannon weighing more than 26,000 pounds onto a gun carriage for testing. (USEPA.)

In 1952, the US Army Corps of Engineers built a battery plant for military contracts north of Foundry Cove. The plant went through several ownerships. Until 1965, wastewater from the plant containing cadmium and nickel was discharged into the Hudson River. Thereafter, it was discharged directly into Foundry Cove through the plant's wastewater treatment system. The pollution generated several phases of EPA Superfund cleanup between 1986 and 1996. (USEPA.)

This photograph shows the huge cylindrical processing tanks that the EPA used to separate water from silt and mud. Along the upper curve of the rail tracks are mounds of contaminated waste that derived from the processing. The dryer mud was then mixed with a cement-like material in order to chemically bind the metals to prevent possible recontamination and to create transportable matter that could be moved to a specialized landfill. (USEPA.)

The Foundry Cove marsh restoration included a long berm to prevent the tide from disturbing the site. A variable amount of sediment was dredged from the cove, and a sandwich-like tarp—two parts canvas and one part clay—was laid on its surface and submerged by sandy loam to allow the regrowth of vegetation and the creation of a wildlife habitat. Monitoring of this successful effort is ongoing. (USEPA.)

Scenic Hudson purchased 87 acres comprising the foundry site and its cove in 1996. In 2001, faculty members and graduate students from Michigan Technological University began a six-year summer field program of research and industrial archaeology at the preserve. This included work, pictured here, on the foundation for the original waterwheel for the blowing engine at the site of the 1827 blast furnace. (Photograph by Jan Thacher.)

A member of the Michigan Tech team works in the stone-lined housing for an eight-foot cylinder for the blowing engine, which forced air into the blast furnace. The tree above the excavation spot is indicative both of the filling in of land and of the natural growth that occurred over most areas of the foundry ruins. (Photograph by Jan Thacher.)

The 1865 office building (page 41) was stabilized during the period of Michigan Tech archaeology and under the direction of Scenic Hudson and the firm Stephen Tilly, Architect. At a corner of the facade, its wall having settled, information is being recorded for an engineering investigation of the foundation, before stabilization. The building was far more deteriorated than it had been 25 years earlier (page 113). (Stephen Tilly, Architect.)

Disassembling was required because of extreme instability at the rear wing, an addition to the original structure. Bricks were removed, labeled, and stockpiled for possible later use at the site. The office building has not reopened; its cupola and bell were removed before major work on stabilization began. The bell is mounted on a boulder at Haldane High School in Cold Spring. (Stephen Tilly, Architect.)

This 300-pounder Parrott rifle bolt, one of four extant, is a type of projectile that had a hardened, flat nose and was used only during the 1863 Charleston siege operations (pages 56–67). Cast at the foundry, such bolts were fired at Fort Sumter from a 300-pounder rifle on Morris Island. (West Point Museum Collection, USMA.)

Pictured at the West Point Ordnance Compound is a Model 1840 forty-two-pounder seacoast cannon manufactured at WPF. Most cannons of this model were employed in coastal defense batteries and were produced at the foundry in 1841 and 1842; but this one was cast in 1845. It is one of three 42-pounders catalogued as survivors and the only one of them made at the foundry for the US Army. (West Point Museum Collection, USMA.)

From left to right are three Parrott rifles, respectively 10-pounder, 30-pounder, and 20-pounder types. The 30-pounder was used in the Charleston siege operations and managed 4,606 shots before bursting in front of the breech band. The midsection of the gun, including the trunnions, is missing. The breech band, immovable because of its weight, rests on the pavement in the foreground. (West Point Museum Collection, USMA.)

One of two 100-pounder Parrott rifles at the West Point ordnance compound is in the foreground. This type of heavy artillery piece saw widespread usage by both the US Army and Navy in the Civil War. The WPF produced approximately 600 of this type beginning in 1861. Late in the war, some 100-pounders were converted to breech-loading rifles for use by the Navy. (West Point Museum Collection, USMA.)

This 1963 photograph shows the damage done by prolonged maritime conditions to this row of 100-pounder Parrott rifles on casemate carriages at Fort Sumter in Charleston Harbor. The fort was rebuilt after the end of the Civil War, and 11 of the original first-tier gun rooms were restored, some fitted with Parrott rifles, as seen here. (Library of Congress.)

Members of the Monitor Center conservation team remove the massive XI-inch Dahlgren smoothbore cannons from the USS *Monitor* turret. Recovered in 2002 off Cape Hatteras, the cannons and turret will be on permanent exhibition at the Monitor Center in Newport News, Virginia, following conservation. Cast by the foundry in 1859, the cannons fired on the CSS *Virginia* in the first clash between ironclad ships (page 69). (Mariners' Museum, Monitor Center.)

Members of Paulson Brothers Ordnance Corp. (PBO) fire a 30-pounder Parrott rifle from a reproduction front pintle barbette carriage during an exercise at Fort McCoy, Wisconsin. The PBO has collected Civil War artillery since 1970 and has fired Parrott rifles at US Army artillery ranges across the United States. (Paulson Brothers Ordnance Corp.)

At Camp Ripley, Minnesota, a PBO gun crew named First Minnesota readies a 30-pounder Parrott rifle for firing. Set here in a siege carriage, the 30-pounder was used for siege and garrison duty throughout the Civil War. The PBO performed live fire exercises yearly from 1975 to 2001. (Paulson Brothers Ordnance Corp.)

The steam-driven beam engine and sugar mill (page 28) at Hacienda la Esperanza, Manati, Puerto Rico, is the only known machinery of its kind to survive. A newly poured concrete foundation has replaced the original brick footing. The cast-iron machinery with the foundry's name and date of manufacture, 1861, in relief has been restored and painted. (Para la Naturaleza, a unit of the Conservation Trust of Puerto Rico.)

The many WPF products on view at American historic sites and museums include this undated signal cannon at the Putnam History Museum. Signal cannons, either on land or aboard ship, were used for such purposes as sounding a salute, warning of danger, or attracting attention. Because they are small, signal cannons are sometimes mistaken for toys. Gunpowder would have been packed into their bores and ignited; they did not fire projectiles. (PHM.)

Two Gothic Revival iron seats were made at the WPF after Gouverneur Kemble (page 14) offered such a gift in 1836 to his writer friend Washington Irving for his porch at Sunnyside, in Tarrytown, New York. Irving requested a design from his neighbor, the painter George Harvey (c. 1806–c. 1876). Seen in a detail from a photograph of about 1903, the seats remain at Sunnyside today. (Library of Congress.)

This undated iron seat replicates those given to Washington Irving, shown on the previous page. It was made by the WPF probably sometime after 1864. Owned by the PHM, it is often placed so that visitors may use it to view John Ferguson Weir's *The Gun Foundry* (page 33) in the museum's West Point Foundry gallery. (PHM.)

Iron furniture manufactured by the foundry in the late 19th century includes this Victorian hat and coat rack with umbrella stand produced in an ornate, curvilinear style popular in the period. This piece and several smaller iron household objects, such as trivets and bootjacks, are also in the collection of the PHM. (PHM.)

This two-thirds scale replica of the Parrott 10-pounder was forged and donated by Norman Champlin, a local blacksmith. It was placed at Cold Spring's former dock area in 1995 by the Veterans of Foreign Wars Post 2362 in memory of American war veterans. This spot has one of the most scenic views of the Hudson Highlands, especially to the north, with Storm King Mountain in the distance. (Photograph by Mark Forlow.)

In the autumn of 2013, Scenic Hudson opened the foundry site as a public park called the West Point Foundry Preserve. Architectural landscaping provides several trails through the property around the foundations of many foundry structures. A metal recreation of a segment of the boring mill's back shot waterwheel stands where the original 36-foot-diameter wooden wheel (page 38) was located. (Photograph by Mark Forlow.)

The Chapel of Our Lady Restoration (1977) was inspired by the foundry's Chapel of Our Lady (1834; page 77) and bears a close resemblance to it. It is ecumenical and used for concerts, weddings, and other functions. This photograph (1990) shows its location facing the Hudson River on a promontory near Foundry Cove. (Photograph by Jan Thacher; PHM.)

This restful spot on the Hudson River, now Foundry Dock Park, is adjacent to the Chapel of Our Lady Restoration and is owned by Scenic Hudson. Railroad tracks once ran from here onto the foundry's dock (page 12). A replica of the tracks is in the foreground. The park opened in 2006 with volunteer help. (Photograph by Mark Forlow.)

BIBLIOGRAPHY

Gillmore, Quincy A. *Engineer and Artillery Operations Against the Defenses of Charleston Harbor in 1863*. New York: D. Van Nostrand, 1865.

Grace, Trudie A. *Around Cold Spring*. Charleston, SC: Arcadia Publishing, 2011.

Holley, Alexander L. *A Treatise on Ordnance and Armor*. New York: D. Van Nostrand, 1865.

IA, *The Journal of the Society for Industrial Archeology*. Vol. 35, nos. 1–2, 2009, published 2012. Theme issue: West Point Foundry, articles by Elizabeth N. Hartnell, Gouverneur Kemble transcribed by Steven A. Walton, T. Arron Kotlensky, Patrick E. Martin, Timothy James Scarlett/Michael Deegan/Renée Blackburn, Dan Trepal, Steven A. Walton, and Alicia B. Valentino.

Melton, Jack W. Jr. Civil War Artillery Projectiles. www.civilwarartillery.com.

Norris, Elizabeth M. "Cold Spring, Hot Foundry: An Archaeological Exploration of the West Point Foundry's Paternal Influence upon the Village of Cold Spring and Its Residents." PhD diss., University of Massachusetts, Amherst, 2009.

Olmstead, Edwin, Wayne E. Stark, and Spencer C. Tucker. *The Big Guns: Civil War Siege, Seacoast, and Naval Cannon*. Alexandria Bay, NY: Museum Restoration Service, 1997

Paulding, J.N. *The Cannon and Projectiles invented by Robert Parker Parrott*. New York: D. Van Nostrand, 1879.

Paulson Brothers Ordnance Corporation. www.pbocorp.biz.

Ripley, Warren. *Artillery and Ammunition of the Civil War*. 4th ed. New York: D. Van Nostrand Reinhold Co., 1984.

Rutsch, Edward S., JoAnn Cotz, and Brian H. Morell. "The West Point Foundry Site, Cold Spring, Putnam County, New York." Unpublished study, 1979. West Point Foundry Archives, Putnam History Museum, Cold Spring, NY.

To the Sound of the Guns: Civil War Artillery, Battlefields and Historical Markers. markerhunter.wordpress.com.

Tucker, Spencer. *Arming the Fleet: US Navy Ordnance in the Muzzle-Loading Era*. Annapolis, MD: United States Naval Institute, 1989.

West Point Foundry Collection and Archives. Putnam History Museum, Cold Spring, NY. www.putnamhistorymuseum.org.

White, John H. Jr. *American Locomotives: An Engineering History, 1830–1880*. Baltimore: Johns Hopkins Press, 1968.

DISCOVER THOUSANDS OF LOCAL HISTORY BOOKS FEATURING MILLIONS OF VINTAGE IMAGES

Arcadia Publishing, the leading local history publisher in the United States, is committed to making history accessible and meaningful through publishing books that celebrate and preserve the heritage of America's people and places.

Find more books like this at
www.arcadiapublishing.com

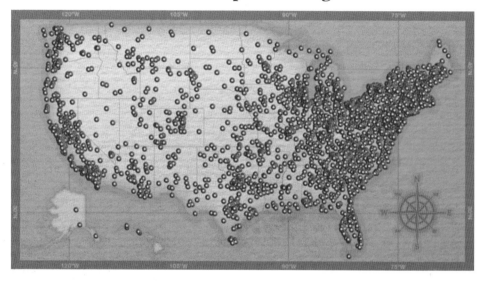

Search for your hometown history, your old stomping grounds, and even your favorite sports team.

Consistent with our mission to preserve history on a local level, this book was printed in South Carolina on American-made paper and manufactured entirely in the United States. Products carrying the accredited Forest Stewardship Council (FSC) label are printed on 100 percent FSC-certified paper.

MADE IN THE